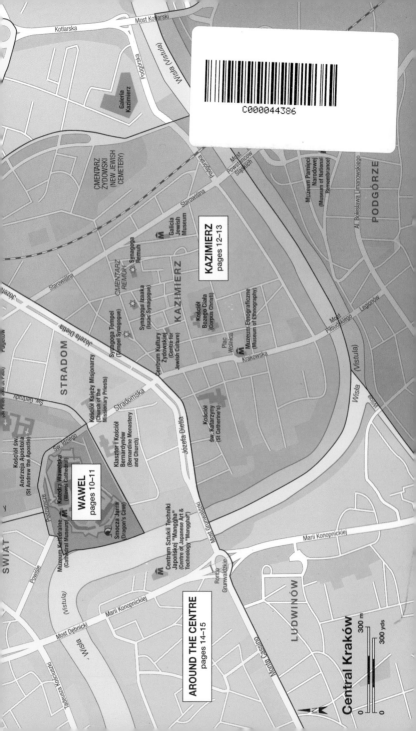

Central Kraków

KOTLARSKA
Most Kotlarski
Galeria Kazimierz
Wisła (Vistula)
Podgórska

CMENTARZ ŻYDOWSKI (NEW JEWISH CEMETERY)

Starowiślna

Most Powstańcow Śląskich

Muzeum Pamięci Narodowej (Museum of National Remembrance)

PODGÓRZE

Al. Bolesława Limanowskiego

Starowiślna

Galicia Jewish Museum

Synagoga Remuh

KAZIMIERZ pages 12–13

CMENTARZ REMUH

Synagoga Izaaka (Isaac Synagogue)

KAZIMIERZ

Synagoga Tempel (Tempel Synagogue)

Centrum Kultury Żydowskiej (Centre for Jewish Culture)

Kościół Bożego Ciała (Corpus Christi)

Muzeum Etnograficzne (Museum of Ethnography)

Plac Wolnica

Krakowska

Most Piłsudskiego

Legionów

STRADOM

Józefa Dietla

Kościół Księży Misjonarzy (Church of the Missionary Priests)

Stradomska

Józefa Dietla

Wisła (Vistula)

Kościół sw. Katarzyny (St Catherine's)

Kościół sw. Andrzeja Apostoła (St Andrew the Apostle)

Klasztor i Kościół Bernardynów (Bernardine Monastery and Church)

Sw. Idziego

WAWEL pages 10–11

Katedra Wawelska (Wawel Cathedral)

Muzeum Katedralne (Cathedral Museum)

Smocza Jama (Dragon's Cave)

ŚWIAT

Powiśle

(Vistula)

Most Grunwaldzki

Centrum Sztuki Techniki Japońskiej "Manggha" (Centre of Japanese Art & Technology "Manggha")

Rondo Grunwaldzkie

Marii Konopnickiej

Most Dębnicki

Wisła

Tadeusza Kościuszki

Marii Konopnickiej

LUDWINÓW

Monte Cassino

AROUND THE CENTRE pages 14–15

0 ___ 300 m
0 ___ 300 yds

N

C000044386

INSIGHT GUIDES

KRAKOW

smart guide

APA PUBLICATIONS **L**

Part of the Langenscheidt Publishing Group

Contents

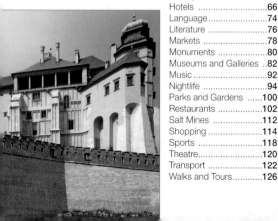

Highlights

▲ **Czartoryski Museum**
A rare opportunity to view a Leonardo da Vinci oil painting.

▼ **St Mary's Basilica**
The spectacular 14th-century church on the Main Market Square is a must-see.

▲ **Auschwitz** Not strictly a highlight, this harrowing camp is a memorial to the horrors of the Holocaust.

▲ **Arka Pana Church**
A modern masterpiece, this hand-built church reveals much about the modern Polish nation.

▲ **Kazimierz nightlife**
Once home to a vibrant Jewish population, this district is now the smartest place in town to drink.

◄ **Wawel** The spiritual home of the nation and the former seat of Polish royalty, Wawel offers a history lesson inside four fortified walls.

Kraków

Kraków has been playing host to powerful kings, illustrious rabbis, gallivanting English stag groups and many others since the establishment of the bishopric of Kraków in AD1000. Twentieth-century tragedies struck hard here, but today, Poland's cultural capital and the seat of its former kings has embraced its role as the country's premier tourist destination.

Kraków Facts and Figures

Population: **756,000**
Area: **327 sq km (126 sq miles)**
Language: **Polish**
Average temperature: Jan **(-5–0°C/23–32°F)**, July **(15–24°C/59–75°F)**
Number of World Heritage Sites: **3 (Old Town, Auschwitz, Wieliczka)**
Religion: **Roman Catholic**
Number of annual visitors in 2007: **7,500,000**
Number of Catholic churches: **120+**
Brands of Polish vodka: **12**
Origin of word 'vodka' (*wódka*): **it is the diminutive for water in Polish and all other Slavic languages**

Kraków's Geography

Situated close to the Slovakian border and just under 300km (186 miles) south of the Polish capital Warsaw at the foot of the Carpathian mountains, Kraków straddles the great Wisła (Vistula) river. The extraordinary 13th-century Old Town to its north is the most popular reason for visiting. Granted Unesco World Heritage status in 1978, the Old Town is unique among major Polish old quarters, being the only one to survive the ravages of World War II, and is worth jumping on a plane for in its own right, although further investigation proves that Kraków is more than just the sum of its medieval urban layout.

The city's modern sprawl houses over 750,000 people and takes in a castle on a hill with a millennium's worth of history, a former Jewish quarter currently reinventing itself as the city's centre of cutting-edge nightlife, crumbling districts punctuated with grand Austro-Hungarian-era architecture and a rich inheritance of communist-built housing estates. Of the last, the unique and must-see Nowa Huta 6 miles (10km) to the east of the city centre, is the only wholly-complete Socialist Realist settlement in the EU and more than worth the 30-minute tram ride to visit. Kraków provides an extensive roll call of contrasting architecture joined together with a marvellous array of green spaces, all of it equally pleasing to culture vultures and backpackers.

Krakovians

Ethnically, Kraków is a predominantly white, Catholic city, with what few foreigners there are coming almost exclusively from neighbouring countries and Western Europe. With its large university, there's a distinctly young feel to the city, although this doesn't stop older generations taking advantage of the city's myriad cultural and nightlife charms. Today, Kraków's industrial heritage has dwindled to almost nothing; instead, an increasingly large percentage of the population work in the service industry, notably tourism.

Below: souvenirs in Cloth Hall.

Above: atmospheric medieval Kraków viewed through Florian's Gate.

Worthwhile Excursions

Neighbouring Zakopane is the country's winter capital and an easy day trip from Kraków. Occasional visitor Vladimir Lenin surely must have approved of the mighty working-class city of Katowice, just over an hour away to the west. Katowice, whose airport does a roaring trade in visitors en route to Kraków, remains one of the country's hidden surprises and is definitely worth a visit when in the area.

When to Visit

There's no best time to visit Kraków as every time of year brings its own set of pros and cons. July and August boast the finest weather, which in turn means that the city is overflowing with visitors, turning much of the time spent in the city into a waiting game of endless queues at the major sights. Christmas and New Year are fun but at times painfully cold. The ultimate compromise is May or September, when there's space to move and the weather is at its most clement.

Although prices have rocketed over the last decade or so, visiting the city is still relatively cheap for Western visitors.

Accommodation, if chosen carefully, can be extremely good value for money, with public transport, museums and dining still affordable for most wallets.

A Vibrant City

It's a sign of the true diversity of Kraków that the city where it's possible to drink merrily all night also gave the world its first non-Italian Pope in over 450 years in the late John Paul II, who represented the Catholic Church globally from 1978 until his death in 2005. Although it is known as a conservative city, it's not hard to see that this is indeed far from the truth. The people in general are more laid-back than their more reserved northern neighbours, a fact reflected in a frenetic café life and continually buzzing late-night scene.

As a cultural centre, Kraków has no national rival. A colourful history of many different peoples has left its mark on the city. With gob-smacking church interiors, art collections to put many Western cities to shame, good theatre, scores of live music events and several diverse festivals, there's more than enough on offer to keep everyone enlightened and entertained.

Main Market Square

Laid out in 1257 and looking much as it did when the bricks were first placed, the city's Main Market Square (Rynek Główny) was, at 220m by 200m (650ft by 650ft), the largest of its kind in Europe for several centuries, and it remains the largest medieval-era square on the Continent. Built to attract merchants of all kinds and to seal the city's trading importance, the Main Market Square features several of Kraków's most famous buildings. In its time the square has witnessed numerous major events but is today literally more pedestrian. Bursting with tourists and ringed with scores of restaurants and cafés, it really is the heart of the city.

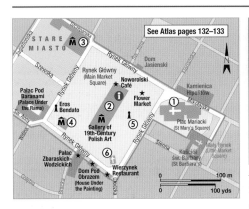

Above: St Mary's Basilica, lit up at night.

ST MARY'S BASILICA AND TOWER

Arguably the feather in the Main Market Square's four-cornered cap is **St Mary's Basilica** ①, a riot of colour inside and worth every penny to enter. Highlights include a painstaking struggle up 239 wooden stairs to see the view from the top of the church's northern-most tower, also famed for its hourly bugle call.

Inside the main building, the High Altar is an absolute must-see, the product of no less than 12 years' work between 1477 and 1489 by the German master Veit Stoss (Wit Stwosz). Entrance to the church is from St Mary's

Square, a small courtyard and popular meeting place joining the Main Market Square and Little Market Square *(see p.9)*.
SEE ALSO CHURCHES AND SYNAGOGUES, P.42

CLOTH HALL

Dominating everything around it is the **Cloth Hall** ②, as old as the square itself, although significantly changed over the centuries. Its contemporary Renaissance look is the work of the 16th-century Italian Giovanni il Mosca. Inside you will find a long corridor selling typical tourist souvenirs, the highly recommended **Noworolski café** where Lenin once

drank coffee and dreamed of revolution, and a planned reopening of the **Gallery of 19th-Century Polish Art** on the top floor.
SEE ALSO BARS AND CAFÉS, P.33; MARKETS, P.78

HISTORICAL MUSEUM OF KRAKÓW

In the far northwest corner of the square stands the main branch of the **Historical Museum of Kraków** ③. Good enough to visit on its architectural merit alone, inside are both permanent and temporary exhibitions related to the history of the city from 1257 until the outbreak of World War II.
SEE ALSO MUSEUMS AND GALLERIES, P.82

Left: lanterns at Cloth Hall.

Although frowned upon by some, the mighty and beautiful horses who earn their oats and carrots pulling carriages laden with tourists around the Old Town appear to be well looked after. A large part of the Main Market Square is taken over with parked carriages complete with two horses which, for around 150zł an hour, will take you anywhere you like within the confines of the former defensive walls.

19th-century Romantic poet who is buried in Wawel. Predating the square by a couple of hundred years is the diminutive **St Adalbert's Church** ⑥, a masterly jumble of styles with a very basic interior that sits a good 2m (6½ft) below the square.

On the square's southern side is the well-known **Wierzynek** restaurant. Serving quality cuisine since the 14th century, the city's oldest restaurant has whisked up dishes for everyone from Steven Spielberg to Fidel Castro.

SEE ALSO CHURCHES AND SYNAGOGUES, P.42; MARKETS, P.78; MONUMENTS, P.80; RESTAURANTS, P.103

OTHER SIGHTS OF INTEREST

A smaller branch of the Historical Museum of Kraków can be found inside the **Town Hall Tower** ④, the only remaining part of the original 14th-century Town Hall, which was demolished by the occupying Austrians at the start of the 19th century. Inside are a few interesting exhibits and another great view from the top of the 68m (223ft) structure.

Nearby is *Eros Bendato*, a partially bandaged head created by the contemporary artist Igor Mitorraj. A refreshing splash of modernity, the inside of the head can be accessed and is a popular place to pose for photographs.

On the other side of the Cloth Hall, the **Flower Market** has been the sole preserve of women traders, often handed down from mother to daughter, since the 16th century. Highly respected, the flower women are responsible for presenting flowers to visiting dignitaries and handing out mistletoe on the square at Christmas.

Next door is the grand **Adam Mickiewicz Monument** ⑤, a statue of the

Right: the *Eros Bendato* sculpture in the square.

Old Town

Kraków's extraordinary Old Town has remained more or less faithful to its original design from when the city first received its charter in 1257. Encased in the green belt of the Planty park, the grid-like Old Town was taken by surprise by the Red Army in 1945 and so avoided the fate of most Polish cities during the Nazi retreat. Home to Europe's third-oldest university and a staggering collection of churches, museums and galleries housed inside some of the finest examples of medieval architecture in Europe, the Old Town's cultural importance was recognised in 1978, when it was entered on the original Unesco World Heritage list.

NORTH

Built in the late 15th century, the **Barbican** ① is where many tourist trails begin. Standing in the far northern part of the **Planty**, it was the key to the city's defence, armed with 130 guns and crowned with seven pointy turrets. Although never tested in war, it remains a symbol of the city, as well as the first hint that you've entered a town of indefinable majesty.

Directly to its south is **Florian's Gate** ②, which Polish kings once passed through en route to Wawel. Recent restoration work has seen its ramparts opened to the public, giving the structure a glistening glow usually associated with assembly-line perfection.

The locals proclaim Kraków as Poland's cultural capital, a claim given credence by a visit to the **Czartoryski Museum** ③.

Among the exhibits is the magnificent *Lady with an Ermine*, one of very few Leonardo da Vinci oil paintings on public display.

Further evidence of Kraków's creative past is to be found inside the **Jan Matejko House**, a tenement which has been left as was from the time it was occupied by the eponymous 19th-century artist. No less important is the **Wyspiański Museum** ④, which honours Poland's greatest Art Nouveau talent with multiple displays, including his far-fetched vision of Wawel.

SEE ALSO ARCHITECTURE, P.26; MUSEUMS AND GALLERIES, P.83; PARKS AND GARDENS, P.100

Below: the Basilica of St Francis is richly decorated.

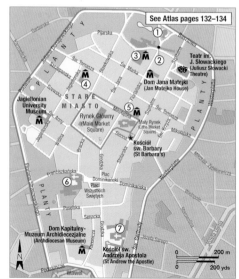

Right: a sculpture adorning the Czartoryski Museum.

Left: St Barbara's Church in Little Market Square.

It's easy to miss a plaque on the eastern outer city wall commemorating Marcin Oracewicz, a sharp shooter who famously rescued the city with a button. In 1768, with the Russians at the gates, Oracewicz rushed to join the defence of the city only to find he'd left his ammo at home. The story goes that the resourceful burgher used his buttons instead, killing the Russian commander with one of them and thus saving Kraków.

EAST
See how Kraków's ruling merchants once lived inside the **Burgher Museum** (Hippolit House) ⑤, a splendid old house filled with period pieces and recreations of quarters inhabited by the city's elite from the 17th century onwards.

Tucked behind the Main Market Square (see p.6) is the suitably named **Little Market Square**. This quiet enclave is notable for the multicoloured apse of **St Barbara's Church**. Further east, the **Juliusz Słowacki Theatre** exemplifies the eclectic style favoured towards the end of the 19th century, and is adorned with allegorical figures, as well as an interior that once caused scandal on account of the erotic nudes depicted in stone and fabric.

SEE ALSO CHURCHES AND SYNAGOGUES, P.42; MUSEUMS AND GALLERIES, P.83

SOUTH
A visit to the **Basilica of St Francis of Assisi** ⑥ takes in the stunning stained-glass creations of Stanisław Wyspiański. Continue further south to reach **St Peter and St Paul's Church** ⑦, which even in this city of churches stands out as something special. Figures

of the Apostles guard the gateway, while the interiors are a riot of pure Baroque extravagance. Next door is the **Church of St Andrew the Apostle**, a more muted effort but renowned for its Romanesque style and boat-shaped pulpit.

Away from the crowds, ul. Kanonicza is a picturesque street that gently curves towards Wawel. It's here you'll find the **Archdiocesan Museum**, whose principal function is to display ecclesiastical relics and commemorate the building's most famous former resident, the late Pope John Paul II.
SEE ALSO CHURCHES AND SYNAGOGUES, P.43; MUSEUMS AND GALLERIES, P.82

WEST
The **Jagiellonian University** is recognised as the third-oldest in Europe, and the **University Museum** celebrates the fact with displays honouring former alumni such as astronomer Nicolas Copernicus. The Gothic archways and elaborate halls are impressive.
SEE ALSO MUSEUMS AND GALLERIES, P.84

Wawel

The impressive collection of predominantly Romanesque, Gothic, Renaissance and Baroque buildings perched on top of the 50m (165ft) limestone hill known as Wawel is the stuff of legend. A settlement has existed on the site for at least 50,000 years, although for the Poles it's the last thousand of those that are of major importance. A symbol of everything Polish and a huge source of pride to the nation, Wawel functioned as the official home of the country's royalty between 1038 and 1596 after the site was vacated by a celebrated if decidedly mythical dragon. Visiting Kraków and not seeing the majesty of Wawel is unthinkable.

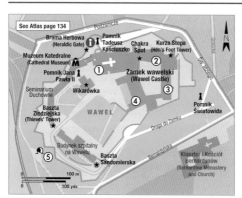

See Atlas page 134

Above: in Wawel Cathedral.

SYNAGOGUES, P.45; MUSEUMS AND GALLERIES, P.85

CATHEDRAL ①

Believed by many to be the most important building in the country, the Cathedral dates back to 1020, although what now stands on the spot owes more to the 14th century and beyond. Truly spectacular, among the many outstanding highlights is the **tomb of St Stanisław** (1030–79), one of the two saints to whom the Cathedral is dedicated. The hefty **Zygmunt's Bell** requires a strapping pair of legs and healthy lungs to reach. Those who do make the climb are rewarded with a great view and the opportunity to pose for a classic Wawel photo opportunity.

Back downstairs, one of the highlights of the Cathedral are the glorious **Side Chapels**. Numbering 18 in all, of these quite stunning works of religious art the most famous is the **Sigismund Chapel**, completed in 1533 and the final resting place of several Polish kings. Many other kings, queens, consorts and assorted national treasures are to be found resting in eternal peace in the **Cathedral Crypts**. Adjoining the Cathedral is the recommended **Cathedral Museum**, opened in 1978 and essential visiting for anyone interested in the Polish Catholic Church.

SEE ALSO CHURCHES AND

CASTLE

The former residential Castle complex started life around the 12th century, although what stands in its place today dates from major rebuilding work in the early 16th century. The vast Renaissance inner courtyard is simply breathtaking, and much of it is open to the public. Of particular note is the **Crown Treasury and Armoury** ②, which is crammed full of treats including the Polish Crown Jewels, the spectacular Szczerbiec coronation

Right: the Wawel complex, even more dramatic at night.

Left: the mighty castle viewed from the street below.

and 12th centuries.

SEE ALSO MUSEUMS AND GALLERIES, P.85

WAWEL WALLS

The hill on which Wawel sits is made of karst limestone and features several underground caves and caverns. According to legend one of them, the **Dragon's Cave** ⑤, was once inhabited by Smok Wawelski, a fearsome dragon slain by Krak, founder of the city. The cave can be visited, and an animated model of the dragon is located outside the exit. On the northern side of the complex is the bronze **Tadeusz Kościuszko Monument**, featuring the military leader and national hero sitting astride his horse.

SEE ALSO CHILDREN, P.40; MONUMENTS, P.81

sword, ornate weapons and reproductions of banners captured from the Teutonic Knights at the 1420 Battle of Grunwald. Also unmissable are the **State Room and Royal Apartments** ③, a veritable labyrinth of corridors and rooms packed with relics and superb works of art.

SEE ALSO CASTLES, PALACES AND HOUSES, P.38; MUSEUMS AND GALLERIES, P.85

ANCIENT WAWEL

According to the Hindus, the northwestern corner of the Castle courtyard contains a rare Chakra Spot. One of only seven (the rest are in Delhi, Mecca, Delphi, Jerusalem, Rome and Velehrad), Chakra spots are said to be part of an energy field connecting all living things. Keep a look out for people who visit specially to gain its life force.

On a more down-to-earth note, **Lost Wawel** ④ exhibits numerous artefacts found on the site over the centuries. Alongside the usual display cabinets is a recommended multimedia show that recreates Wawel as it was during the 10th

Not content with being widely considered Kraków's leading artistic genius, Stanisław Wyspiański, who spent his childhood in a house close to Wawel, set out in 1904 to redesign the castle after it was vacated by the occupying Austrian army. With the help of the local architect Władysław Ekielski (1855–1927), Wyspiański's so-called 'Wawel-Akropolis' featured several additional buildings, towers, churches and even an ampitheatre, in an attempt to create a vision of the former glories of the once grand Polish state. Failing health and a lack of funds saw the design never leaving the drawing board, although a small model was made in the 1980s and can now be seen in the museum that bears the artist's name. *See Museums and Galleries, p.85.*

Kazimierz

Founded in 1335 as a trade rival to neighbouring Kraków, Kazimierz became home to the city's Jewish population a century later following their expulsion from Kraków. After the ravages of World War II, Kazimierz became something of a slum, but was brought back to life with the release of Steven Spielberg's multi-Oscar-winning 1993 film *Schindler's List* and has since emerged as the beating heart of Kraków's bohemian social life. Nowadays it presents a beguiling tangle of synagogues, galleries, legends and cafés that more than gives the Old Town a run for its money. Kazimierz is also the obvious start and end point for any Jewish-related visit to the city.

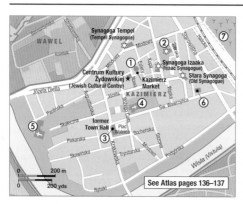

See Atlas pages 136–137

The tomb of 16th-century Rabbi Remuh is visited by Jews the world over, and the scraps of paper left behind are entreaties from pilgrims. Entrenched in Hassidic legend, it's said the tomb only survived the vandalism of the Nazis after a group of them were struck by lightning while attempting to dismantle it. Thereafter, the Nazis left it well alone.

AROUND PLAC NOWY

Detractors of Kazimierz point accusingly at the area's increasing gentrification, though they'd do well to visit **plac Nowy** ①, a public square framed by peeling tenements. Here the pulse of Kazimierz can be measured, particularly in the umpteen bars lining its flanks. It's from such a vantage point that visitors can view the central **Kazimierz Market** building, itself dating from 1900 and used in the inter-war period as a ritual Jewish slaughterhouse for poultry. However, you'll find the real market action directly around this rotunda, where traders gather to hawk everything from farm

produce to second-hand clothes to pre-war antiques. On the corner of the square lies the **Jewish Cultural Centre**, a one-stop shop which allows visitors to gather pamphlets, peruse literature or view concerts and exhibitions. Across

from plac Nowy you will find the **Isaac Synagogue**, built in 1644, which has benefited from 1990s renovation work, although for sheer wow factor don't miss the intricate Moorish interiors of the nearby **Tempel Synagogue**.

SEE ALSO CHURCHES AND SYNAGOGUES, P.46, 48; MARKETS, P.78

AROUND UL. SZEROKA

For many, ul. Szeroka is where the Jewish heritage trail begins, and no place of worship is more famed than the **Remuh Synagogue** ②, which has conducted services since 1553. The cemetery behind it survived the Nazis because many of the tombs that are now visible

Left: the Tempel Synagogue's splendid interiors.

extensive redesign undertaken between 1733 and 1742. In 1079 St Stanisław was murdered at the altar on the orders of the king, and parts of his body were thrown into the font outside. Today, water from the fountain is said to have healing powers. The Pauline Church **Crypts** provide further reason for visiting, with the fine vaulted basements featuring the sarcophagi of luminaries including the local artist Stanisław Wyspiański and the Nobel Prize-winning author Czesław Miłosz. SEE ALSO CHURCHES AND SYNAGOGUES, P.47

were then sunken in the ground, and it was only post-war excavations that led to their discovery. At the southern end of ul. Szeroka is the **Old Synagogue**. Thought to date from 1407, this brick construction houses a small exhibition documenting the area's Jewish history. SEE ALSO CHURCHES AND SYNAGOGUES, P.47

AROUND PLAC WOLNICA
Plac Wolnica was originally Kazimierz's market square, and while it's now just a quarter of its original size, it's still worth visiting for the Renaissance-era former town hall in the middle. Since 1911 the building has been host to probably the best **Museum of Ethnography** ③ in the country. To

the northeast of the square, the **Corpus Christi Church** ④ is one of the great Gothic glories of Kraków. Its 70m (230ft) tower is an unmissable landmark in the area. SEE ALSO CHURCHES AND SYNAGOGUES, P.46; MUSEUMS AND GALLERIES, P.86

TOWARDS THE RIVER
The **Pauline Church** ⑤ has been a site of worship since the 11th century, although it owes its current Baroque form to an

TO THE EAST
A misnomer if ever there was one, the **Galicia Jewish Museum** ⑥ is in fact a photographic gallery focusing on sites of Jewish interest in their current, derelict state. The overall effect is deeply evocative, and well paired with a visit to the nearby **New Jewish Cemetery** ⑦. Established in 1800, the cemetery proves the perfect place to ponder the area's past. SEE ALSO MONUMENTS, P.81; MUSEUMS AND GALLERIES, P.86

Right: poignant images at the Galicia Jewish Museum.

13

Around the Centre

The better-known parts of the city are surrounded by a plethora of lesser districts that, although holding no particular fascination on their own, collectively make up a substantial contribution to the sights and sensations Kraków has to offer. These sights are spread out in all directions and feature everything from churches to a zoo and even a museum containing a rare World War II Spitfire in Polish livery; visiting them requires a little pre-planning. Taking advantage of the city's superb tram system and wearing a comfortable and sturdy pair of shoes is highly recommended. For more information on getting around the city, *see Transport, p.124.*

NORTH

The area north of the Old Town is more than worth a visit. Just north of the Barbican *(see p.8)* is the mighty **Grunwald Monument** ①, celebrating not only one of Poland's major historical achievements but also one of the most famous battles of medieval Europe. Immediately north of the monument is **St Florian's Church**, which can be traced back to the 12th century but is now predominantly Baroque. The starting point of the former coronation route, this church is named in honour of the Polish patron saint of fire-fighters and chimney sweeps. A fair old hike west is the **History of Photography Museum**. Small and a little threadbare, the

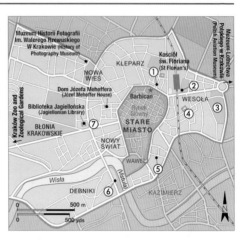

museum is said to be the only one of its kind in the country and features some fine old prints of the city, as well as the occasional exemplary exhibition.

SEE ALSO CHURCHES AND SYNA-GOGUES, P.48; MONUMENTS, P.80; MUSEUMS AND GALLERIES, P.87

EAST

For sheer eccentricity, **Celestat** ②, a museum dedicated to men whose king owns a silver chicken *(see box, opposite)*, is hard to beat. Less eccentric are

the city's **Botanical Gardens** ③, a pleasantly bucolic retreat not far from the Old Town and the venue for a series of outdoor classical concerts every summer. Nearby is the towering **Jesuit Church** ④, dating from the beginning of the 20th century yet looking and feeling much older than it really is. The church features designs from a range of local artists including sculptor and Auschwitz survivor Xawery Dunikowski (1875–1964).

Way out east is the **Polish Aviation Museum**, a

Left: the café at Manggha offers Japanese specialities.

Above: explore Sarmatism at the Celestat museum.

Left: stunning stained glass at the Mehoffer Museum.

is the magnificent Gallery of 20th-Century Polish Art.

Nearby, get a breath of fresh air at the large **Błonia** park before heading back towards the Old Town via the **Mehoffer Museum**, the former home of one of the country's leading Modernist painters. The house has been wonderfully preserved and features many original works of art. The nearby **Jagiellonian Library** is housed in two modern wings, both of them of architectural interest and containing thousands of books, manuscripts and prints.

Right out in the sticks at the end of an interesting bus ride is the **Kraków Zoo and Zoological Gardens**, surprisingly good for Eastern Europe and a great opportunity to get away from it all for a few hours.
SEE ALSO CHILDREN, P.41; MUSEUMS AND GALLERIES, P.87, 88; PARKS AND GARDENS, P.101

Shrouded in conflicting theories as to its precise origins, Sarmatism relates to the former lifestyle of the *szlachta*, Poland's nobility, who between the 16th and 19th century adopted the practices of the Sarmatians, a warlike tribe from north of the Black Sea from whom the Poles mistakenly believed at one time they were descended. Favouring ostentatious oriental clothing, horsemanship and splendid handlebar moustaches, Polish Sarmatism lives on today in the shape of the bizarre Fowler Brotherhood, whose Celestat museum can be found in a small park just east of the train station. *See also Museums and Galleries, p.86.*

curate's egg of a collection where communist-era fighter jets rust outside and some truly beautiful machines are lovingly looked after inside a couple of hangars.
SEE ALSO MUSEUMS AND GALLERIES, P.86; PARKS AND GARDENS, P.100

SOUTH
Housed inside the city's former **Natural History**

Museum, the **Kraków Aquarium** ⑤ is the brainchild of an American expat entrepreneur with a penchant for all things scaly. A good one for the kids, the Art Nouveau building is equally worth a visit.

Just over the river and further proof that Kraków is more than just churches and old buildings, the intriguing **Manggha** ⑥ offers a large nod to the Orient, namely with a series of exhibits from the private collection of the late Japanophile, Feliks Jasienski.
SEE ALSO CHILDREN, P.41; MUSEUMS AND GALLERIES, P.87

WEST
The austere-looking, highly recommended **National Museum of Art** ⑦ hides three very different but equally rewarding exhibitions. Alongside historical military and decorative arts

Podgórze and Płaszów

The districts of Podgórze and Płaszów, which lie immediately south of the city centre and directly across the river, often find themselves linked together on account of their geography and disturbing history during World War II. These districts are home to over half a million people; the tendency to assume they were born of the Industrial Age couldn't be further from the truth. The area south of the river boomed under the stewardship of the Austrians, but its history predates that, as is proved by the existence of the Krakus Mound. Incorporated into Kraków in 1915, Podgórze in particular is now regarded as one of the city's up-and-coming neighbourhoods.

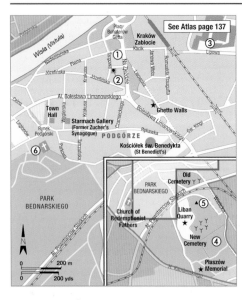

Above: a tribute to Holocaust victims posted on a remaining section of the Ghetto wall.

March 2010, but subject to repeated delays, the building houses Kraków's most long-awaited tribute to the Holocaust. You can also visit the abandoned **Liban Quarry**, used by Steven Spielberg as a backdrop for *Schindler's List*. This Industrial Age plant was once used by the Nazis, and its craggy peaks and rusting furnaces make for an eerie walk. Less sinister, the **Starmach Gallery** is found inside a 19th-century Jewish prayer house, and today hosts an avant-garde gallery every bit as interesting as the building it's found in.

SEE ALSO MONUMENTS, P.80; MUSEUMS AND GALLERIES, P.88, 89

JEWISH PODGÓRZE

In 1941, Kraków's Jews were moved to a ready-sealed Ghetto in Podgórze, with plac Zgody becoming the heart of their 'prison without a roof'. Rechristened **Ghetto Heroes' Square** ① after the war, it is overlooked by the **Museum of National Remembrance** ②. It's here that Tadeusz Pankiewicz and staff, the only Gentiles allowed to remain, ran the Pharmacy Under the Eagles during wartime, supplying the imprisoned Jews with aid. Their efforts, and the fate of the Ghetto, are commemorated in this museum. Little remains of the Ghetto walls, although sections can still be viewed on ul. Lwowska and ul. Limanowskiego.

Set beyond these, to the northeast, is **Schindler's Factory** ③. Currently scheduled to open in

Left: the sombre Płaszów Memorial.

Pan Twardowski, who once cast spells on the site of Bednarski Park and the Krakus Mound, was a sorcerer born in Kraków in the 16th century.

Legend has it that Twardowski's greed saw him enter a pact with the devil, whereby in exchange for a fortune Satan would be entitled to his soul should Twardowski ever enter Rome. The deal backfired on Twardowski when he stepped into a local inn called Rome, where he was promptly abducted by the devil and banished to the moon. According to the fable, Twardowski sits there to this day along with his only companion, a spider, watching the Krakus Mound from afar.

PŁASZÓW

Head south for **Płaszów Concentration Camp** ④, a windswept park where all traces of Nazi atrocity have been erased. In operation from 1942, the camp grew to cover over 80 hectares (198 acres), with Jews and Poles used as slave labour in the surrounding quarries. The real point of attraction here is the 1964 **Płaszów Memorial**, ringed by a ditch once used to execute some of the 8,000 who are estimated to have died here.

SEE ALSO MONUMENTS, P.81

PODGÓRZE OF LEGEND

In the 1930s, archaeologists unearthed 'the oldest structure in the city'. The **Krakus Mound** ⑤ is a 16m (52ft), man-made mound allegedly erected in the 7th century by the local inhabitants in honour of Prince Krak, the founding father of the city.

St Benedict's Church is one of the great anomalies of Kraków, open just once a year and built on top of the site of a former pagan temple. **Bednarski Park** is one of the finest examples of early 20th-century landscaping. However, before its reinvention as a horticultural heaven it was known

Below: the Krakus Mound.

for its connection with Pan Twardowski, a sorcerer who once practised his black arts amongst the groves and trees.

CATHOLIC PODGÓRZE

Completed in 1909, **St Joseph's Church** ⑥ is the best-known landmark in the area, complete with an 80m (262ft) tower and an altar cross inspired by Wit Stwosz's work in St Mary's Basilica *(see p.42)*. It's not the only church of note however. Take, for example, the **Church of Redemptionist Fathers**, whose 1908 completion was funded by the sale of 25,000 pictures of the *Mother of God of Eternal Help*. Also worthy of a look are the **Old** and **New Cemeteries**, thick with trees, moss-covered stones and the weather-worn tombs of esteemed locals.

SEE ALSO CHURCHES AND SYNAGOGUES, P.49

Nowa Huta

B uilt from the ashes of World War II, Nowa Huta (New Steelworks) is everything Kraków's Old Town isn't. A vast Socialist Realist gift from the Soviet Union and constructed to house 100,000 newly born communist citizens, Nowa Huta was a massive social and architectural experiment. It was centred around an enormous steel plant that would help reconstruct a country devastated by war, but the ideology of Nowa Huta soon backfired, with the town developing into a hotbed of working-class Catholic dissent against the authorities. One of Poland's stranger sightseeing opportunities, Nowa Huta offers an extraordinary experience just 30 minutes from the centre of Kraków.

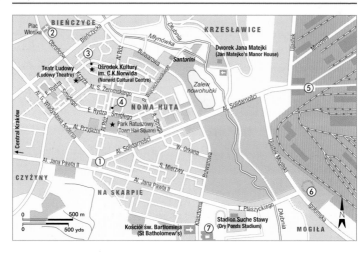

RONALD REAGAN CENTRAL SQUARE

This giant palm of a hand with radiating roads for fingers is now known as **Ronald Reagan Central Square** ①, and although this small green space surrounded on three sides is impressive, a look at the original plans for Nowa Huta show that there was to be much more in store for the town. Looking like nothing else you've ever seen, the square is the first port of call on any trip to Nowa Huta.

SEE ALSO ARCHITECTURE, P.27

THE CENTRE

Nowa Huta has grown considerably over the decades, much of it lacking in the original architectural vision. The original centre, though, remains fairly untouched and is, with the exception of a few new shops, cars and advertising boards, pretty much as it was. The **Town Hall Square** is a lovely little green park, alive during the summer with a combination of children and retired men playing chess in the shade. The **Teatr Ludowy** *(see box, opposite)* was built just after the end of the Socialist

Realist phase but is still worth a look at, notably for the pompous chandeliers. Meanwhile, the **Arka Pana Church** ② is without a doubt on a par with Poland's greatest churches. Completed in 1977, the church was built entirely by hand and hides several extraordinary things inside.

Hidden away in a housing block, the **Norwid Cultural Centre** is fairly unremarkable, but for fans of art, a trip upstairs to view the works by the famous Kraków Group is more than worth the climb.

Left: St Bartholomew's Church in Mogiła.

Nowa Huta's small Teatr Ludowy has an extraordinary reputation worldwide. A leading focal point of the avant-garde for over 50 years, perhaps its most interesting innovation has been its Therapy Through Art *(Terapia Przez Sztukę)* programme. Working with orphans, drug addicts and other marginal groups, the theatre's most famous experiment was to bring together two local warring groups of punks and skinheads to produce a radical production of *Romeo and Juliet. See also Theatre, p.121.*

ferent diversion, complete with original furniture, paintings and memorabilia. SEE ALSO ARCHITECTURE, P.27; MUSEUMS AND GALLERIES, P.89

Guarded by a tank, the **Museum of the Armed Act** ③ ranks among Kraków's finest museums. The low-budget feel is more than made up for by the treasures hidden within. For a quick history lesson, visit the **Nowa Huta Museum** ④, which also houses the local Tourist Information Centre. SEE ALSO CHURCHES AND SYNAGOGUES, P.49; MUSEUMS AND GALLERIES, P.90; THEATRE, P.121

SENDZIMIR STEEL-WORKS AND AROUND

Originally named after Lenin, the **Sendzimir Steelworks** ⑤ requires plenty of advance warning for a visit, or the help of a recommended tour guide. Hidden away in the middle is the **Solidarity Remembrance Room**, a small

collection of items commemorating Nowa Huta's contribution to the downfall of communism.

At about 15m (50ft), the **Wanda Mound** ⑥ dates from around the 7th century. Nobody's quite sure what it was built for, with some arguing a pagan temple and others some kind of astronomical clock.

The **Jan Matejko Manor House**, the former home of one of the city's most celebrated painters (1838–93), is a wildly dif-

MOGIŁA AND AROUND

Incorporated into Nowa Huta in 1973, the small settlement of Mogiła boasts two splendid churches. The monumental **St Wenceslas Church and Cistercian Monastery** ⑦ has been around since the 13th century, albeit with major additions over the years. **St Bartholomew's Church** was originally built in the 15th century and is the only wooden church in the city. SEE ALSO CHURCHES AND SYNAGOGUES, P.50

Right: the monumental Sendzimir Steelworks.

Katowice

That most foreigners are aware of Katowice's existence is down to two things, an airport and a mind-boggling history of pollution, but there is much more on offer at this city, 90 minutes from Kraków. A child of the Industrial Revolution, what had hitherto been a backwater community was transformed with the discovery of coal, and by 1897 had grown into a city. Situated in the heart of Silesia, the story of Katowice resembles a game of Risk, chronologically passing between Bohemians, Habsburgs, Germans, Poles, Nazis then finally, in 1945, Poland again. Refreshingly off the tourist radar but more than worth a visit, working-class Katowice is one of Poland's true surprises.

CITY CENTRE

Familiarise yourself with the history of the region by visiting the **Silesian Museum** ①, a venue which holds an outstanding collection of 19th- and 20th-century Polish art, including five original paintings by Stanisław Wyspiański. Katowice was a political hot potato after World War I, with possession fiercely disputed between Poles and Germans alike. Gustaw Zemła's imposing **Silesian Insurgents' Monument** ② was unveiled in 1967 and honours the Poles who took part in the three uprisings between 1919 and 1921.

West of the train station lies the slightly down-at-heel **plac Wolności**, and in it a monument to the Red Army, one of only a handful surviving in sushi-age Poland. Katowice's very own UFO can be found just north of the centre. Known as the **Spodek** ③, this controversial, flying saucer-shaped concrete concert hall was completed in 1971 and is one of the architectural marvels of the communist years.
SEE ALSO ARCHITECTURE, P.27; MUSEUMS AND GALLERIES, P.90

Above: the dramatic Silesian Insurgents' Monument.

SOUTH OF THE STATION

The 60m (197ft) **Cloud Scraper** may look a little underwhelming at first glance, but this 1934 residential building was only the second skyscraper to be built in Poland, and until 1955 it was the tallest building in the country.

Another particularly brave piece of architecture is the **Silesian Parliament** ④, notable for being the largest building in the country when it was completed in 1929. More evidence of Katowice's obsession with size comes with the **Christ the King Cathedral** ⑤, Poland's largest ecclesiastical build-

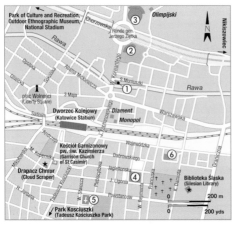

Right: a Katowice tenement.

Left: the Cloud Scraper.

Ten kilometres (6 miles) south of Katowice lies the town of **Tychy**, better known as the home of Tyskie, Poland's premier export lager. With a history that goes back nearly 400 years, the brewery is open for free tours, has a great museum, and includes a beer-tasting after.

OTHER SIGHTS OF INTEREST

Technically in neighbouring Chorzów, the 620-hectare (1,550-acre) **Park of Culture and Recreation** claims top ranking as Europe's largest park, and aside from a decent zoo and small planetarium, it also features the highly recommended outdoor **Upper Silesian Ethnographic Park**. Also located here is the **National Stadium**, opened in 1956. Tours of the 60,000-capacity stadium take in superb and disparate minutiae including Socialist Realist artwork and changing rooms. SEE ALSO MUSEUMS AND GALLERIES, P.90

ing, even without the 38m (125ft) dome which was originally planned to sit on top. The mostly bland interior is very much a triumph of size over style, so for aesthetic pleasures head to the **Garrison Church of St Casimir**, best known for its stained glass and dazzling Art Deco interior.

The **Katowice Historical Museum** ⑥ offers a complete A–Z of everything you could possibly want to know about the city, and

includes reproductions of typical local residences from select periods in the last century. A green interlude can be found at the **Tadeusz Kościuszko Park**. Opened in 1925, the park includes an English-style garden, the lovely wooden church of **St Michael the Archangel** and a well-preserved Soviet soldiers' cemetery among other sights. SEE ALSO ARCHITECTURE, P.27; CHURCHES AND SYNAGOGUES, P.50, 51; MUSEUMS AND GALLERIES, P.90; PARKS AND GARDENS, P.101

INDUSTRIAL KATOWICE

One surprise addition to the Unesco World Heritage list is **Nikiszowiec**, a workers' commune constructed between 1909 and 1911. Designed to be self-sufficient, the housing estate was considered ground-breaking when it was first completed.

Rising indiscreetly over Tadeusz Kościuszko Park are the chimney stacks of the Wujek mine. Established in 1899 and once used as a labour camp for World War I prisoners, the mine hit world headlines on 16 December 1981 when nine coal miners were killed as tanks sought to enforce martial law on a strike-hit Poland. A monument unveiled 10 years later by Lech Wałęsa commemorates the event, and incorporates a wooden cross which has stood there since 1981.

Zakopane

Complete with its own wooden architectural style of buildings, ski slopes galore and a clump of restaurants selling artery-clogging meat dishes eaten to the beat of in-house oom-pa-pa ensembles, the small mountain resort of Zakopane shot to fame in 1873 when local doctor Tytus Chałubiński began promoting the town for its supposed health-giving properties. Nestled at the foot of the mighty Tatra mountains, a popular destination for both hikers and winter sports enthusiasts, Poland's winter capital offers a few surprisingly good sights and functions both as a magical day trip less than two hours from Kraków and a destination in its own right.

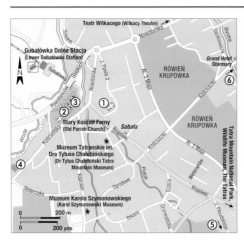

Above: the rustic St Mary of Częstochowa Church.

UL. KRUPÓWKI

Zakopane's main pedestrian thoroughfare, ul. Krupówki offers visitors the chance to eat traditional grilled meat, gape at human statues and generally bump into other people doing the same thing. Two sights along it of note are the 1899 **Holy Family Church** ①, containing a wealth of folk art and religious icons, and the **Dr Tytus Chałubiński Tatra Mountain Museum**, complete with a stuffed bear in the entrance and a highly recommended series of displays focusing on the local culture and wildlife.

SEE ALSO CHURCHES AND SYNAGOGUES, P.51; MUSEUMS AND GALLERIES, P.91

AROUND TOWN

Completed in 1851, the small wooden **St Mary of Częstochowa Church** ② and neighbouring **Na Pęksowym Brzysky Cemetery** ③ are positively packed with interest, the former being a fine example of a traditional Polish rural church complete with folk art motifs, the latter being the final resting place of many of the town's former illustrious citizens. On the other side of town, the

Tatra Mountain National Park Wildlife Museum provides a good introduction to the many rare species to be found inhabiting the local area.

SEE ALSO CHURCHES AND SYNAGOGUES, P.51; MUSEUMS AND GALLERIES, P.91

ZAKOPANE AND THE ARTS

Historically a traditional retreat for Polish artists, Zakopane offers several exemplary places to learn about the creative side of life in the region. The **Zakopane Style Museum** ④ inside the **Willa Koliba** was built in 1894 in the classic Zakopane style by Stanisław Witkiewicz, whose wayward and

Left: a traditional Zakopane wooden house.

Like many locals before and after her, Zakopane-born Helena Marusarzówna (1918–41) learned to ski practically before she could walk. The winner of numerous national skiing titles at an early age, when war came to Zakopane the young Górale woman applied her mountain skills to the fight against the Nazis by smuggling people and mail over the Carpathians and into Hungary. In March 1940 Marusarzówna was captured by the Hungarian police and handed over to the Gestapo who tortured her for several months without success before executing her the following year. Her grave can be found in the cemetery next to the St Mary of Częstochowa Church.

eccentric son, known to the world as Witkacy (1885–1939), is represented upstairs with a number of bizarre paintings.

The **Karol Szymanowski Museum**, in an unassuming residential street, celebrates the local pianist and composer (1882–1937) who incorporated folk music into his intriguing compositions. Alternatively, visit the **Kornel Makuszyński Museum** ⑤, the former home of Poland's version of A.A. Milne, Koziołek Matołek, whose stories about an adventurous mountain goat charm children to this day.

Władysław Hasior (1928–99) was a local artist and stage designer whose strange mixed-media works fill the extraordinary **Władysław Hasior Gallery** ⑥.

The **Witkacy Theatre**, named in honour of Zakopane's wackiest son, puts on experimental theatre, has a great café, and features some magnificent murals outside based on the artist's life and works. SEE ALSO ARCHITECTURE, P.27; MUSEUMS AND GALLERIES, P.91

THE TATRAS

The northernmost and highest part of the Carpathian mountain range, the Tatras cover a substantial part of the area around Zakopane and neighbouring Slovakia and are a hugely popular destination. Famed for both hiking and winter sports, the mountains around to Zakopane offer everything from brown bears to eagles to all-night après-ski sessions in wooden cabins. A spot of particular interest is **Mount Giewont**, a three-peak mountain with a 15m (50ft) steel cross at the top of its highest point, at 1,894 metres (6,214ft). Popular with serious hikers,

climbers and Catholics alike, the mountain is perilously dangerous. All trips to the mountains should be undertaken with the greatest of care. **Morskie Oko** (Eye of the Sea) is the largest lake in the Tatras. Set amidst spectacular scenery, the lake is cut off from roads, requiring a long walk or horse-drawn cart to get there. SEE ALSO SPORTS, P.119

Below: a view of the Tatras.

A–Z

In the following section Kraków's attractions and services are organised by theme, under alphabetical headings. Items that link to another theme are cross-referenced. All sights that are plotted on the atlas section at the end of the book are given a page number and grid reference.

Architecture

It's no exaggeration to say that very few places in Europe can match Kraków and its immediate surroundings for architectural diversity. Spared the fate of every other major Polish city during World War II, its historical Old Town survived almost intact, and boasts one of the most spectacular ensembles of medieval buildings anywhere in the world. The strife that both the city and the country has undergone countless times over the centuries has also, somewhat ironically, left its mark in the shape of scores of other classic architectural styles, from the Art Nouveau of the city centre to the visionary Socialist Realist buildings of neighbouring Nowa Huta.

KRAKÓW

MEDIEVAL

Kraków's Old Town is almost exclusively given over to the medieval era, with every street boasting several stunning examples of the age. Dating from Romanesque times, the diminutive **St Adalbert's Church**, consecrated in 997, and **Church of St Andrew the Apostle** are excellent examples of this style, while Gothic glories galore await at the top of ul. Floriańska. The Renaissance period is perhaps best exemplified by the **Cloth Hall**, its roof topped with foul-faced gargoyles, whilst the glories of the Baroque stage in Kraków's development can be witnessed at the overly extravagant **St Peter and St Paul's Church**.

SEE ALSO CHURCHES AND SYNAGOGUES, P.44, 45, 47; MARKETS, P.78

Florian's Gate

ul. Pijarska and ul. Floriańska; tram: 2, 4, 5, 12; map p.133 D3
Arguably no other structure in Old Town represents its history and culture than the predominantly Gothic Florian's Gate and the tower through which it passes. Dating from the 14th cen-

tury and built as part of the city's original defence system, the square, 33.5m (110ft) tower topped with a 17th-century Baroque roof is the last remaining of the eight originally built. Named for St Florian, whose image adorns the southern side; 2009 saw the upper ramparts opened to the public for the first time, complete with a small exhibition.

ART NOUVEAU

At the turn of the 20th century, Kraków was in the grip of a new artistic movement with strong nationalist overtones, known as *Młoda Polska* (Young Poland). Influenced by several styles including Impressionism and Art Nouveau, local artists including Stanisław Wyspiański and Józef Mehoffer stamped a new identity on Kraków not just on canvas but also in stone. The finest examples of the architecture of the *Młoda Polska* era, which are strikingly

Left: Florian's Gate.

Left: Art Noveau detail.

60m (197ft) steel-frame building is considered to be the finest example of Polish Functionalist architecture. The much sought-after residential address is easily missed due to its now insignificant size and dirty appearance, but for fans of classic inter-war buildings this one is unmissable.

Spodek

al. Korfantego 35
Built between 1964 and 1971 and a fine, if somewhat controversial, example of communist-era tensegrity architecture, Spodek (Saucer), as it's known as by locals, is a 246,624 sq m (2,655,000 sq ft) UFO lookalike made from reinforced concrete and designed to host everything from sporting events to rock concerts. The doors open sporadically, other than for events.
SEE ALSO MUSIC, P.93

ZAKOPANE
Zakopane Style Museum (Willa Koliba)

ul. Kościeliska 18; tel: 18 201 3602; www.muzeumtatrzan skie.pl; Wed–Sat 9am–5pm, Sun 9am–3pm; admission charge
This building was completed in 1894 to an original design by Stanisław Witkiewicz (1851–1915) and is still considered to be one of the finest examples of a style that now predominates much of Zakopane's skyline. Blending classic wooden mountain architectural design with local folk-art motifs, the house is decorated on the outside with scores of intricate carvings.
SEE ALSO MUSEUMS AND GALLERIES, P.91

About 3km (2 miles) southeast of Katowice's city centre, **Nikiszowiec** (German, Nikischau) is a post-industrial masterpiece currently awaiting Unesco World Heritage status. Built between 1908 and 1911, the small red-brick housing estate once sheltered local miners and their families and included a post office, bakery, hospital, schools and the neo-Baroque St Anne's Church, which is worth a look inside.

similar to Art Nouveau, can be found lining ul. Piłsudskiego, ul. Retoryka and ul. Smoleńsk just to the west of the Old Town.

House Under the Singing Frog

ul. Retoryka 1; tram: 2, 3, 8, 15
A building of particular interest, being a strong example of this historic revival style. Designed by Teodor Talwoski (1857–1910), the building features numerous whimsical flourishes, including a fiddle-playing frog that adorns its upper levels.

NOWA HUTA

SOCIALIST REALISM

The only place to see a complete Socialist Realist town inside the EU, Nowa Huta is a treat for fans of communist-era architecture. Although much of it never received the full-on treatment originally planned, what remains is both substantial and, in some instances, bizarre.

Of the many things to see, the two outstanding sights are plac Centralny (Ronald Reagan Square), built in 1949 and, at the far northeastern end of al. Solidarnośc, the two administrative buildings belonging to the former Lenin, now Sendzimir, Steelworks. Pompous and amusing, the entrances to both structures are open to the public.

KATOWICE
Cloud Scraper

Hidden away just south of the train station at ul. Żwirki i Wigury 15 is the *Drapacz Chmuri*, or Cloud Scraper. Completed in 1934, the

Auschwitz

From its inception in 1940 to its liberation in 1945, Auschwitz I and its surrounding sub-camps would claim centre stage in the Nazis' Final Solution to the 'Jewish Problem'. In little less than five years an estimated 1.1 to 1.5 million people (900,000 thought to be Jews) were systematically murdered here as the Nazis exploited science for slaughter in their quest for Aryan supremacy. For many, Auschwitz represents the nadir of the death camps, a place where radical racial theory was allowed to culminate into one of the largest systematic acts of genocide ever known, and a place where humanity was taken to the brink.

GETTING THERE

Poles know Auschwitz by its Polish name, **Oświęcim**, and that's the name you'll need to be looking for on all maps. The 75km (47-mile) westward journey from Kraków is a feasible day trip, with two trains that run from early morning. The journey time is approximately 90 minutes and costs just over 10zł. For the latest train timetables, refer to www.pkp.pl. From the station the camp is well signposted, and walking the remaining distance should take no more than 20 minutes. Several taxis wait outside the station, and most will have meters specially fitted to take advantage of tourists.

Travelling by minibus is far preferable to travelling by train, and you'll find several departing from the lower level of Kraków's bus station. There'll usually be a bus on the hour, although once the tourist season starts in late spring their frequency rises consider-ably. The journey takes 90 minutes, and most buses pass directly outside the main gates of Auschwitz I. You'll need to pay the driver directly on boarding, which currently costs around 10zł. Birkenau can be found less than 3km (2 miles) north of the main camp. From mid-April until the end of October the two camps are linked by an hourly bus service. Taxis wait throughout the year outside Auschwitz I, costing anything from 15–30zł.

AUSCHWITZ I

ul. Więźniów Oświęcimia 20, Oświęcim; tel: 33 844 8000; www.auschwitz.org.pl; Dec–Feb 8am–3pm, Mar–Nov 8am–4pm, Apr–Oct 8am–5pm, May–Sept 8am–6pm, June–Aug 8am–7pm (closed 25 Dec, 1 Jan, Easter Sunday); free (introductory film 3.50zł)

Perhaps no other image is more symbolic of the Holocaust than the inscription which hangs above the main gates of Auschwitz, *Arbeit Macht Frei* (Work Makes You

Above: a forbidding building at the main camp.

Free). For those imprisoned, this century-old nationalist slogan was one more exhibition of German cynicism and the final hoax in a system hell-bent on perpetrating, then hiding, one of the biggest crimes in the history of civilisation.

The beginnings of Auschwitz were far from sinister. In 1916, 22 brick barracks were built to house migrant workers, and for years these operated as a quasi refugee camp complete with a school, orchestra and theatre. Later these were

Left: bleak Birkenau, the largest of the Nazis' camps.

While Auschwitz is primarily known as a place of Jewish suffering, a huge number of others were also persecuted and murdered here. Particularly close to Polish hearts is the story of the Franciscan friar Maksymilian Kolbe (1894–1941), a convicted resistance activist who broke ranks to volunteer his life for that of a Polish prisoner selected for death. Kolbe was sentenced to death by starvation in cell 20 of the Death Block, although after two weeks of survival he was eventually executed by phenol injection to the heart. He was beatified in 1971 and canonised by the late John Paul II on 10 October, 1982. The man he saved, former army sergeant Franciszek Gajowniczek, lived until 1995.

claimed by the Polish army to house the garrison stationed in Oświęcim, and it was only in 1940 that the camp caught the eye of the Nazi leadership.

For months, Himmler had been hunting for a suitable area to turn into a concentration camp, and while the barracks of Auschwitz were run-down and situated around swampy ground, they had the benefit of excellent train links. On 27 April Himmler signed the decree ordering the construction of a concentration camp, and on 14 June the first transport of predominantly Polish prisoners arrived. Himmler visited the following year on 1 March, and was so impressed with what he saw that the immediate expansion of the camp was ordered.

If you're not on a guided tour of Auschwitz then do buy the official pamphlet. Available for 4zł, this foldaway is crucial if you're to follow the prescribed route. With this guidebook in

hand, visitors will walk through the countless exhibitions that are now housed in the former barracks. In the first such building various evidence of atrocities can be found as well as cans of the notorious gas used in the extermination process. Most indicting of all is some 7 tonnes of human hair destined to be turned into everything from socks to rope.

As grisly as this introduction is, little prepares visitors for what lies next. Set behind protective glass are tonnes and tonnes of

loot hoarded by the Nazis and discovered by the Soviets on liberation on 27 January 1945. The toothbrushes, false limbs, prayer shawls and suitcases make for powerful viewing, followed by the high impact of the collection of children's toys and clothing. In the eyes of the Nazis, all these items could be recycled for the benefit of the Third

Below: inmates' personal effects are displayed at Auschwitz.

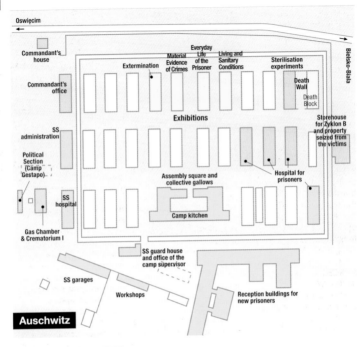

Oświęcim

Commandant's house

Commandant's office

SS administration

Political Section (Camp 'Gestapo')

SS hospital

Gas Chamber & Crematorium I

Extermination

Material Evidence of Crimes

Everyday Life of the Prisoner

Living and Sanitary Conditions

Sterilisation experiments

Death Wall

Death Block

Exhibitions

Storehouse for Zyklon B and property seized from the victims

Assembly square and collective gallows

Hospital for prisoners

Camp kitchen

SS guard house and office of the camp supervisor

SS garages

Workshops

Reception buildings for new prisoners

Bielsko-Biała

Auschwitz

Commemorating the fate of those killed in Auschwitz has proved a contentious issue which has divided both Polish and Jewish communities for several decades. Matters came to a head in 1984 when a chapter of Carmelite nuns opened a convent close to the site, a move which aggravated Jewish leaders. The premises were vacated in 1993, but a 26m (85ft) cross left over from Pope John Paul II's 1979 visit remained. Appeals to remove this crucifix in the late 1990s were met with fury by Catholic activists, and a further 300 protest crosses soon mushroomed around. The removal of these, but not the papal cross, was finally agreed following tense dialogue after years of feuding.

Reich. And so it goes, barrack after barrack of sobering, hard-hitting viewing. Learn of day-to-day living conditions in dormitories that have been faithfully reconstructed, of the doctors who experimented on their patients, and of the tortures prisoners would undergo.

Block 11, nicknamed 'the Death Block', is particularly chilling. Tourists file past the SS courtroom where summary two-minute trials were held, before peering into rooms containing torture instruments. The cellars are even more horrifying. It's here that the Nazis first experimented with gas, killing 600 Soviet soldiers and 250 Poles in September 1941. It's also here where 'special prisoners' were held in tight 'star-

vation cells' or 'standing cells', where four prisoners would be placed in chambers measuring no more than 90cm (8ins) across.

Having completed the first part of the tour, visitors then make an abrupt U-turn to walk through barracks now designated as exhibitions of national suffering. Designed and overseen by nations affected by Nazi terror, these include some dusty, damp and outdated displays and largely pointless pieces of artistic statement, but others, however, should not be missed, such as the stark and evocative Dutch contribution, or the no-holds-barred approach taken by the Hungarians.

Right: rail tracks cut through Birkenau camp.

Right: piles of suitcases are a poignant reminder of 1.1–1.5 million victims' final journey.

Just outside the camp perimeter, past the excellent exhibition detailing the persecution of the Roma, lies the gas chamber. In operation from 1941 to 1942, this was the final stop for thousands of Soviet and Jewish prisoners, with up to 350 corpses cremated daily in the crematoria to the side. Fittingly, with the gas chamber visible, the camp's first commandant, Rudolf Hoss was hanged at the gallows on 16 April 1947.

AUSCHWITZ II (BIRKENAU)

While there is less to see at Birkenau than at its parent camp, its size and solitude render it deeply moving. Constructed towards the end of 1941 and opened in March 1942, Birkenau became the largest of all the concentration camps, and at its height was home to over 100,000 inmates.

Visits begin at the main gate, where a guard tower has wide views over the former death factory. The majority of buildings were destroyed during the Nazi flight, and much of what you see before you is nothing more than the skeletal brick chimney stacks which remained long after the wood barracks were burned to the ground. A few remain, however, directly to the right. Originally used as stables, here up to 1,000 prisoners at a time were incarcerated in tights conditions, with lice and disease the direct consequence.

Running directly through the middle of the camp are

train tracks, where prisoners were unloaded from cattle wagons before being selected for work or death. Some of those chosen for the former would have found themselves in the women's camp to the left side of the tracks, and many of these stone buildings remain open to the public. Both time and vandalism have taken their toll, yet it's still possible to identify genuine wartime murals amidst the shadows and smashed masonry.

Visits reach a climax with the huge 1967 monument *To the Victims of Auschwitz*. Flanking the wreaths and plaques are the twisted remains of the crematoria and gas chambers, and while fenced off they leave in no doubt the scale of the slaughter. Further on, visitors can visit Birkenau's one proper permanent exhibition, found in what was dubbed the 'sauna'. It's in here prisoners selected for work would first face delousing, registration and then the tattooing of their arms. Today the building is filled with mementoes from this time, including personal effects, photographs and family heirlooms buried in the ground by prisoners.

Bars and Cafés

Allegedly, no other city in the world can boast a higher concentration of bars than Kraków's Old Town; whether or not you choose to believe this piece of local lore is neither here nor there. The fact is visitors are spoilt for choice when it comes to refreshment of a liquid nature, and part of Kraków's endless charm lies in exploring its bountiful bar scene. The line between bars and cafés remains blurred, and nowhere is this truer than in the Kazimierz district, where shadowy locales, buried in nostalgia and candlelight, transform into havens of hedonism as evening progresses.

OLD TOWN

Bunkier
pl. Szczepański 3a; tel: 12 431 0585; Sun–Wed 9am–2am, Thur–Sat 9am–3am; tram: 2, 3, 4, 12; map p.132 B3
Part of the recommended **Bunkier Sztuki** art gallery; take your pick and knock back espressos, wines and spirits in the small and intriguing jumble sale-looking area inside or out on the large, year-round Planty-located terrace. Service aside, which can be both indifferent and occasionally forgetful, this is one of the top spots of its type in town.
SEE ALSO MUSEUMS AND GALLERIES, P.83

Above: Camelot café is a local institution.

Camelot
ul. Św. Tomasza 17; tel: 12 421 0123; daily 9am–midnight; tram: 2, 4, 7, 10; map p.133 C3
The title for Kraków's best café is hotly disputed, but Camelot must surely be in contention. Featuring whitewashed walls and folk puppets, the highlight of this long-enduring café is undoubtedly the made-

on-the-day desserts, many of which threaten to topple the tables with their size. Like much of the centre, this student favourite is increasingly a tourist hang-out, but one which never lacks charm.

English Football Club
ul. Mikołajska 5; tel: 12 421 0149; www.efckrakow.pl; daily 1pm–1am; tram: 2, 4, 7, 10; map p.133 D2
Whether you want to join them or avoid them, knowledge of this Brit boy paradise can make or break a holiday. Filled with

framed football shirts and private beer taps, this cellar bar is most definitely one for the lads.

Irish Mbassy
ul. Stolarska 3; tel: 12 431 0221; www.irishmbassy.com; Mon–Thur noon–1am, Fri–Sat noon–3am; tram: 2, 4, 7, 10; map p.133 C1
This three-floored Irish mega-pub was wrought from a former medieval prison, and the exquisitely restored Gothic brickwork can still be seen throughout. Not by the largely British clientele who

Left: whatever your tipple, there's a bar in Kraków for you.

among the most reliable in town. Tables disappear as night rolls on and the punters move in, and it's not uncommon for evenings to end as day breaks outside.

Noworolski

Rynek Główny 1/3; tel: 12 422 4771; www.noworolski.com.pl; daily 9am–midnight; tram: 2, 4, 7, 10; map p.132 C2

Join an antique-looking crowd in Noworolski, a local institution in business since 1912. Imperial-looking with its colonnades and red-and-white wedding-cake interior, this place is known as much for its associations with Lenin as it is for its desserts. It's in here that a pre-revolution Vladimir would entertain both wife and mistress, sometimes simultaneously, while waiting for couriers like Stalin to arrive with despatches from the east.

Piękny Pies

ul. Sławkowska 6a; www.piekny-pies.pl; daily noon–late; tram: 2, 4, 7, 10; map p.132 B3

Nights can be riotous in

With summer come the beer gardens, and while the most obvious place to enjoy a sunshine pint is the Main Market Square, it's by no means the best. Or the cheapest. For atmosphere alone, head for the courtyards of ul. Bracka in the Old Town, where the carousing lasts until long into the night. Rather oddly, the English Football Club has taken charge of a glorious garden running off ul. Św. Krzyza, while for something more sophisticated, enjoy sunset drinks on the rooftop terraces of the Stary and Copernicus hotels.

gather though, their thoughts more focused on swaggering in front of umpteen sports screens while vigilant staff pour perfect pints of Guinness and resist endless saucy chat-up lines.

Jama Michalika

ul. Floriańska 45; tel: 12 422 1561; www.jamamichalika.pl; Mon–Thur 9am–10pm, Fri–Sat 9am–11pm; tram: 2, 4, 7, 10;

map p.133 D3

A voluptuous-looking effort featuring a velvety-green decor and a stiff air of Secession-era elegance, it's within these wood-panelled confines that the *Młoda Polska (see Architecture, p.26)* movement was born over a century back. The café was once home to the legendary cabaret act Zielony Balonik.

Nic Nowego

ul. Św. Krzyża 15; tel: 12 421 6188; www.nicnowego.com; Mon–Thur 7am–2am, Fri 7am–late, Sat 10am–late, Sun 10am–2am; tram: 2, 4, 7, 10; map p.133 D2

Locals and foreigners happily coexist in Nic Nowego, an Irish-owned venue which buzzes from dawn. Floor-to-ceiling windows and a pavement terrace lend this spot a modern café atmosphere, while a tactful design sidesteps any shamrocks or leprechauns. Indeed, it's only the hospitality and Guinness which allude to Ireland, while the menu is

Below: inside wood-panelled, historical Jama Michalika.

Above: there's no shortage of places to grab a coffee and cake.

the Beautiful Dog, a cult venue which packs out the darker it gets. With sticky tables and swampy toilets it's immediately obvious where the proprietor's priorities lie, fun ahead of style, and that's never truer than during the weekend, when DJs perform downstairs to a youthful audience that'll be unconscious by dawn. Forget the haphazard design, stick to bottled beer and you'll find this courtyard bar is legendary in standing.

Scandale Royale

pl. Szczepański 2; tel: 12 422 1333; www.scandale.pl; Sun–Thur 7.30am–midnight, Fri–Sat 7.30am–2am; tram: 2, 3, 4, 8; map p.132 B3
With a purple-and-violet design, Scandale Royale is emblematic of modern-day Kraków, attracting a cocktail crowd who've grown out of the dungeon-like bars so prominent in the area. Svelte and mod-

ern, the touches here include a show-stealing chandelier and shattered-glass flooring, as well as designer drinks fixed by black-clad staff.

U Louisa

Rynek Główny 13; tel: 12 617 0222; www.ulouisa.com; Sun–Wed 11am–1am, Thur–Sat 11am–5am; tram: 1, 3, 6, 8; map p.132 C2
There's an almost Arthurian spirit in U Louisa, a classic Kraków cellar whose vaulted stone chambers unravel to reveal

a subterranean drinking labyrinth. Big-screen sport serves the purpose of attracting the groups, while the long tables and German import lager add to an animated atmosphere of beer-hall revelry.

KAZIMIERZ
Alchemia

ul. Estery 5; tel: 12 421 2200; www.alchemia.com.pl; daily 9am–3am; tram: 7, 9, 11, 13; map p.135 E1
Dilapidated and dog-eared Alchemia's skin faults are easily overlooked. A true bastion of Kazimierz cool, this venue has been attracting playwrights and artists – some hailed, most failed – ever since its inception a decade ago. Interior arrangements consist of scruffy antiques and faded photographs, though often go unnoticed thanks to the near-Stygian blackness. Eccentric and atmospheric, not least when live bands entertain downstairs. Peculiar for Poland, this place features bar service only.

Eszeweria

ul. Józefa 9; tel: 0668 413 068; daily 11am–2am; tram: 7, 9, 11, 13; map p.135 D1
Looking like a condemned building with decorations commandeered from a rubbish dump, this is what contemporary Kazimierz is all about. Ignoring the poor choice of available beer, everything else inside this bohemian masterpiece is spot on, from the excellent little beer garden to the interesting characters you're bound to meet inside. Eszeweria also hosts regular live music and cinema events.

Right: bohemian hangout Alchemia is full of atmosphere.

Les Couleurs

ul. Estery 10; tel: 12 429 4270;
Mon–Fri 7am–midnight;
Sat–Sun 8am–midnight; tram:
7, 9, 11, 13; map p.135 E1
Even the old French
posters littering the walls
don't detract from what's
one of the best café-bars
in the city. With a rough
and ready approach to
furniture and a clientele
composed of Kraków's
bookish, arty and just
plain eccentric set, Les
Couleurs is good for both
daytime coffee and drink-
ing the night away.

Miejsce

ul. Estery 1; tel: 0783 096 016;
www.miejsce.com.pl; Sun–Wed
10am–1am, Thur–Sat 10am–
2am; tram: 7, 9, 11, 13; map
p.135 D2
There's an edge of
Berlin chic to Miejsce, an
industrial-looking, white-
walled space with a heavy
injection of retro. Illuminated by lava lamps and
mismatching lights, the
mushroom-look tables
come occupied by media
types with laptops flipped
open and black coffee by
their side. Second-hand
geek fashion is very much
the vogue in this open-
late, gay-friendly haunt.

Moment

ul. Józefa 26; tel: 0668 034
400; www.momentcafe.pl;
Sun–Thur 8am–2am, Fri–Sat
8am–3am; tram: 7, 9, 11, 13;
map p.135 E1
A vintage Vespa parked
on the pavement
announces Moment, a
slick Kazimierz space with
out-of-sync clocks and an
urbane crowd of local hip-
sters. Chessboard flooring

and design-store furnish-
ings make it a welcome
break from the car-
boot-sale interiors of
neighbouring venues.

Propaganda

ul. Miodowa 20; tel: 12 292
0402; daily 11am–3am; tram:
3, 6, 8, 10; map p.135 D2
Murky doesn't begin to
describe Propaganda, yet
peer behind the smoky
gloom and you'll discover
a remarkable collection of
communist cast-offs res-
cued from the glory years
of the People's Republic.
Half dive-bar, half living
museum, it hosts a griz-
zled crowd taking hard-
core refreshment amid
frayed posters and flags,
as well as random jumble-
sale extras such as broken
televisions and a rusting
motorbike.

Singer

ul. Estery 20; tel: 12 292 0622;
Sun–Thur 9am–3am, Fri–Sat
9am–6am; tram: 7, 9, 11, 13;
map p.135 E1
Classifying this local masterpiece is tricky business.
By day you'll discover a
charming little café,
cloaked in dusky half-light
and scattered with flicker-
ing little tea candles on

antique sewing machines.
As night sets a different
creature emerges, one
which sees tables utilised
for dancing as wannabe
bohemians dressed in
shabby-cool fashion enjoy
one of the most random
music policies in Kraków.

Szynk

ul. Podbrzezie 2; tel: 0695 415
066; www.szynk.pl; daily
1pm–midnight; tram: 3, 6, 8,
10; map p.135 D2
Totally local, utterly
friendly and completely
unfashionable, Szynk is

> Ever since low-cost carriers
> started flying to Kraków, the city
> has become something of a
> weekend playpen for touring
> British males, never more so
> than in the height of summer.
> The knock-on effect has been an
> increase in the number of strip
> clubs, noise and men in silly out-
> fits, something which, unsurpris-
> ingly, the locals haven't taken to
> kindly. While a ban on visiting
> stags has been discussed, it
> looks unlikely, so in the mean-
> time those wishing to enjoy
> Kraków's less cultured side can
> do so in any number of foreign-
> aimed bars, including the
> legendary Irish Mbassy and the
> English Football Club (see p.32).

Right: enjoy coffee in trendy
surroundings at Miejsce.

Above: on sunny days, locals flood the beer gardens.

where to head once you've overloaded on tourist-trap Kraków. The only accents here are Polish, and while the interior of rusty rakes and rural detritus won't win prizes the beer certainly will. Sourced from the local Amber Browar, you'll be lucky to find a better tipple anywhere else.

Whilst other European nations race to pass anti-smoking legislation through their respective parliaments, the good news for smokers visiting Kraków is that the issue isn't even being discussed in Poland. While there are clearly good reasons for banning smoking in all public places, there are also many who consider the loss of this ancient rite in Europe's bars and cafés to have put something of a dampener on their social lives. Whilst even the neighbouring Lithuanians, champion smokers if ever there were any, have outlawed the habit, smokers looking for extra incentive to visit Poland will be delighted to learn that for at least the short-term future, the bars, cafés and restaurants of the nation remain full of smoky clouds.

AROUND THE CENTRE
CK Browar
ul. Podwale 6/7; tel: 12 429 2505; www.ckbrowar. krakow.pl; Mon–Thur 9am–2am, Fri–Sat 9am–4am; tram: 2, 3, 4, 8; map p.132 A2
Kraków's sole micro-brewery attracts every social category, from tracksuited teens to foreign beer enthusiasts, with a cellar location and sports broadcasts amplifying the resultant din to almost uncomfortable levels. Copper brewing barrels glisten in the distance of this dark, narrow bar, and provide plenty of redeeming factors to visit this often over-populated venue. The house beers, from which there's usually a choice of four plus, are outstanding.

Stary Port
ul. Straszewskiego 27; tel: 12 430 0962; www.staryport. krakow.pl; Mon–Wed 9am–1am, Thur–Fri 9am–3am, Sat noon–3am, Sun noon–1am; tram: 2, 3, 8, 15; map p.132 A2
For a place as safely land-locked as Kraków it comes as a bit of a surprise to find that it not only has its very own nautical-themed bar but that it's a hugely popular one at that. Bursting with sailing-related paraphernalia and packed most evenings with a beguiling mix of students and lovers of sea shanties, this peculiar recommendation also plays host to the city's annual sea shanty festival.
SEE ALSO FESTIVALS, P.56

PODGÓRZE AND PŁASZÓW
Drukarnia
ul. Nadwiślańska 1; tel: 12 656 6560; www.drukarnia-podgorze.pl; Sun–Thur 9am–1am, Fri–Sat 9am–4am; tram:

7, 9, 11, 13; map p.137 D2
There is life beyond Kazimierz, and Drukarnia is the proof. Set across the river, this bar is at the forefront of the Podgórze renaissance, with the occasional jazz performances a particular highlight. Kraków pubs like to celebrate the peculiar, and this one comes with an unlikely printing-press theme cropping up amid the bare bricks and exposed piping.

NOWA HUTA
1949
os. Urocze 14; tel: 12 644 1162; www.1949club.pl; daily noon–9pm tram: 4, 16, 17, 21
A celebration of Nowa Huta in the form of a themed café, this fairly recent addition to the district's limited choice of places to go out has no alcohol licence (or a proper coffee machine for that matter), but it is

8am–4am, Sat 9am–5am, Sun 2pm–midnight
Attracting everyone from skater boys to students, reaching the bar in the subterranean Negresco involves a maze-like route through half-lit chambers. Obstacles come from random fittings accrued from thrift stores and flea markets, while the barman's CD collection points to an overwhelming obsession with hip hop and gangsta rap.

Sky Bar

ul. Uniwersytecka 13; tel: 32 601 0100; www.qubus hotel.com; Mon–Fri 6pm–2am, Sat–Sun 4pm–2am; 10zł for non-guests
The quintessential lofty hotel bar, as seen the world over. At 27 floors high, Katowice's Sky Bar is worth the 10zł entrance charge if you're not staying here for the magnificent view of the city, if little else. Decorated with a few model aeroplanes and featuring the occasional DJ, it's all really about what's on the other side of the windows here, which, it must be said, is quite a sight.

ZAKOPANE
Café Piano

ul. Krupówki 63; daily 3pm–midnight
Escape the Polka-playing shepherds posing for photographs on every other street corner and duck into zany Café Piano. Looking like a Japanese restaurant that ran out of money, this Zakopane classic attracts a predominantly local crowd who gather to enjoy a few drinks and, if they arrive early enough, to take pole position on one of the bar stools fashioned from swings and hanging from the ceiling.

Paparazzi

ul. Galicy 8; tel: 18 206 3251; www.paparazzi.com.pl; Mon–Fri 4pm–1am, Sat–Sun noon–1am
A more picturesque location you will not find. Set next to a burbling stream, the outdoor seating is a summer highlight, while in other seasons take solace inside among darkened booths decorated with paparazzi snaps of screen icons. This is the classiest place in town, with cocktails that blow the competition sideways.

worth popping in if only for the photographs and Nowa Huta-related knick-knacks strewn about the place.

KATOWICE
Archibar

ul. Dyrekcyjna 9; tel: 32 206 8350; www.archibar.pl; Mon–Thur 10am–midnight, Fri–Sat 10am–3am, Sun 2–10pm
Owned by the local Architects' Union, which may or may not explain the radical interior design, this is the top cocktail spot in town for thinking drinkers. Located in the small pedestrianised area close to the train station, Archibar is a good place to visit after looking around town and before heading back to the metropolis.

Negresco

ul. Wawelska 6; tel: 0693 523 663; Mon–Thur 8am–1am, Fri

Below: a lively jazz session at Podgórze's Drukarnia.

Castles, Palaces and Houses

Kraków's hugely important place in the hearts of the nation as the home of the country's former kings and queens is reflected in its castle at Wawel, beautifully restored and, during the height of the holiday season, packed to bursting with visitors from both home and abroad. The city's wealthy history has also left its mark, with scores of grand houses each trying ostentatiously to outdo the other. Several of the more interesting ones, including the following, are open to the public and well worth a peep inside. *See also Museums and Galleries, p.82.*

OLD TOWN

Bishop Erazm Ciołek Palace

ul. Kanonicza 17; tel: 12 429 1558; www.muzeum.krakow.pl; Tue–Sat 10am–6pm, Sun 10am–4pm; admission charge; tram: 3, 6, 8, 10; map p.134 C3

Built between 1503 and 1505 on the whim of Bishop Erazm Ciołek (c.1475–1522), this salmon-pink palace recently reopened as a museum showcasing several permanent exhibitions, including the recommended *Art of Old Poland from the 12th to 18th Century* and *Orthodox Art of the Old Polish Republic*. This second collection of sacral art, including works of Veit Stoss, won't thrill all, but the setting most certainly will.

Enlarged by Ciołek's successor, architectural features include Gothic pillars in the entrance hall and a Renaissance portal. Once used as a prison and police station by Austrian authorities, the 18th-century frescoes in the Hall of Virtues are particularly impressive.

Burgher Museum (Hippolit House)

pl. Mariacki 3; tel: 12 422 4219; www.mhk.pl; Wed–Sun 10am–5.30pm; admission charge; tram: 1, 3, 6, 8, 18; map p.133 D2

An often overlooked museum next door to St Mary's Basilica, this recommended little gem speaks volumes about the former history of the city's merchant classes. Its location, size and internal magnificence give a clear indication of how the other half lived from the 17th century until the time of Polish independence in 1918. Predominantly Renaissance in style on the outside, the interior has seen many changes over the centuries, a fact that really adds something to the items on display.
SEE ALSO MUSEUMS AND GALLERIES, P.83.

WAWEL

Wawel Castle

www.wawel.krakow.pl; 6am–sunset; free, admission charge for inner attractions; tram: 3, 6, 8, 10; map p.134 B2

With a history going back a thousand years, Wawel Royal Castle, as it's officially known, is the highest-ranking monument in Poland. Starting life as a castle in the 9th century,

Left: in the courtyard at Wawel Castle.

Two extraordinary architectural anomalies of note lie either side of the main entrance to the former Lenin (now Sendz-imir) Steelworks in Nowa Huta. Considered to be among the finest examples of Socialist Realist architecture in Poland and dating from the first decade after the end of World War II, the two buildings, officially known as Building S and Building Z, are littered with tiny spires and crenellations and is referred to as the Doge, after its palatially grand exterior. With details stolen directly from the architectural classics of Italy and, to a lesser extent, Silesia, the interiors are no less impressive, although gaining access can be problematic. Those with a real interest should make early enquiries at Nowa Huta's Tourist Information Centre (see p.19).

Left: the Burgher Museum contains fascinating curios.

SEE ALSO MUSEUMS AND GALLERIES, P.85

this magnificent ensemble of buildings housed the first Piast kings before growing in size and stature to become the masterpiece it is today. Brimming with towers, hidden gardens and the spectacular Renaissance courtyard, much of the site is open to visitors for free, although recent years have seen numbers balloon to such proportions that large queues in the height of summer are very much the norm. There are numerous attractions to visit inside the complex.

AROUND THE CENTRE
Villa Decius
ul. 28 Lipca 17a; tel: 12 425 3638; www.villa.org.pl; tram: 15, 18

Hungarian-born Justus Decius (Jost Dietz) arrived in Kraków in 1508 and within a short space of time had become one of the big players in town. He became a confidant of Jan Boner, founder of the salt mines in Bochnia and Wieliczka, and much of the vast wealth he earned was spent on this palace. Remodelled over the years, this Renaissance

gem is admired across Poland as one of the grandest aristocratic residences in the country, with signature arched balconies rising up on three storeys.

Used as a barracks during World War I, Nazi HQ in the next war, and a tuberculosis hospital in the peace that followed, by the 1970s Villa Decius was little more than a ruin. An extensive restoration programme was launched after the fall of communism, and in 1996 this building was reopened to the public as, among other things, a concert and conference venue. The manicured park surrounding it includes a side building housing two hotels and a gallery featuring the work of sculptor Bronisław Chromy (born 1925).

Below: elegant decor at the Burgher Museum.

Children

Kraków and the surrounding area boast plenty of attractions for children, although the great majority of places are still geared towards Polish-speakers. Kids being kids however, language barriers in these cases tend to be less problematic, with children quickly mixing together and communicating in any way they can. The city itself has several places that engage both mind and body, of which the most interesting are listed below. Outdoor-loving children will be particularly enthralled by the options available a couple of hours to the south in the mountain resort of Zakopane.

WAWEL
Dragon's Cave
Wawel; tel: 12 422 5155; www.wawel.krakow.pl; daily 10am–5pm; admission charge; tram: 3, 6, 8, 10; map p.134 B2
A 25 million-year-old limestone cave is the setting for one of Kraków's most famous legends. It's here that *Smok Wawelski*, or the Wawel Dragon, once lived and who, after years of terrorising the locals, was finally killed by none other than Krak, the equally legendary founder of the city. Buy a ticket (3zł at the time of writing) from the machine outside the entrance and explore the monster's lair. A life-size model of the dragon can be found outside, which breathes fire for anyone with a mobile phone who sends the SMS message 'smok' to the number 7168.

HiFlyer Polska
Bulwar Inflancki; daily 10am–8pm; admission charge; tram: 3, 6, 8, 10; map p.134 B1
In a huge white hot-air balloon on the stretch of grass next to the river between Wawel and the Pauline Church, these 15-minute stationary rides 150m (490ft) above the city have become one of the major attractions in Kraków. Queues can get rather long during the height of the summer, so be prepared for a wait.

KAZIMIERZ
Bajkoland
ul. Podgórska 34; tel: 0608 41 1154; www.bajkoland.pl; Mon–Sat 10am–9pm, Sun 10am–8pm; admission charge; tram: 7, 9, 11, 13
A small play area with expert supervision on the upper level of Galeria Kazimierz, close to the cinema and food hall, this is the perfect place to leave the smaller members of the family, giving the grown-ups a chance to do some quality shopping in one of the best malls in the city.

City Engineering Museum
ul. Św. Wawrzyńca 15; tel: 12 421 1242; www.mimk.com.pl; Tue–Sun 10am–4pm; admission charge; tram: 7, 9, 11, 13; map p.137 D3
As well as the large hangar full of brightly coloured old vehicles, the top draw for children inside this exemplary (for Poland anyway) museum is the Fun and Science exhibit, featuring all manner of pulleys, levers and small experiments for kids to interact with and learn the basics of science and technology. Particularly interesting is the electricity demonstration which attaches two electrodes to a cucumber and shows the small voltage it generates on a screen.

Another option for entertaining children is to take one of the summer boat trips along the Wisła river. Excursions last from 30 minutes or so to several hours, with many boats offering food and drink. Find them all moored close to Wawel. The friendly young girls in sailor hats working for each boat and walking around trying to get customers will be only too happy to tell you more about the trips.

Above: Kraków's compact size is ideal for exploring with kids.

SEE ALSO MUSEUMS AND GALLERIES, P.86

AROUND THE CENTRE
H Jordana Park
al. 3 Maja 11; bus: 134
The best outdoor playground in the city, immediately west of the National Museum of Art and just north of the bus stop needed for the zoo; you could combine the two.
SEE ALSO PARKS AND GARDENS, P.101

Kraków Aquarium
ul. Św. Sebastiana 9; tel: 12 429 1049; www.aquariumkrakow. com; Mon–Fri 9am–10pm,

Sat–Sun 9am–9pm; admission charge; tram: 3, 6, 8, 10; map p.135 D3
Housed inside the city's former Natural History Museum and still containing one or two former relics, the Kraków Aquarium is just what Poland has been waiting for. Surplus to the snakes, turtles, monkeys and other beasts living inside are banks of touch-screen information stands for the ultimate in cutting-edge learning.

Kraków Zoo and Zoological Gardens
ul. Kasy Oszczędności Miasta Krakowa 14; tel: 12 425 3551; www.zoo-krakow.pl; daily 9am–6pm; admission charge; bus: 134
One of Eastern Europe's better zoos, a trip here is guaranteed to keep children amused for hours.
SEE ALSO PARKS AND GARDENS, P.101

Park Wodny
ul. Dobrego Pasterza 126; tel: 12 616 3190; www.park wodny.pl; daily 8am–10pm;

Left: the fire-breathing Wawel Dragon.

bus: 159, 172, 501, 5021
A large pool, lots of slides, climbing walls and much more besides.

ZAKOPANE
If you decide to take the kids to Zakopane for the day and are travelling on the bus, do remember that it's a two-hour journey with not much to see out the windows for most of the trip. You'll need something to keep everybody entertained until you get there.

Pony Trekking
At the top of the town's funicular railway, a favourite in itself, the little hamlet of Gubałówka has a few paddocks along the main path full of well-looked-after ponies, most of which can be hired for short trips in the countryside, or a walk around the paddock.

Skiing
www.zakopane.pl
Of the 34 ski runs in the town, several are geared towards novices and children. Ski passes are cheap, and, if you don't mind the slightly chaotic way things are run, very good value.

Below: Kraków Zoo is home to a wide range of animals.

Churches and Synagogues

Poland is a deeply religious, predominantly Catholic country, and nowhere is this more evident than in Kraków, where the streets of the Old Town bristle with the penguin forms of nuns and priests and the peel of church bells. Yet whilst splendid and extravagant, Kraków's places of worship are more than just photographic backdrops. Churches like Wawel Cathedral and St Mary's Basilica sing of glories past, whilst the silence of the synagogues are a poignant epitaph to the region's murdered Jews.

MAIN MARKET SQUARE

St Adalbert's Church

Rynek Główny; tel: 12 422 8352; Mon–Sat 7.30am–6pm, Sun 1.30–6pm; free; tram: 1, 3, 6, 8; map p.132 C2

One of Kraków's first churches and the oldest building found in the Main Market Square, St Adalbert's was built on the spot where St Adalbert supposedly once conducted a sermon in 995. This tiny church is a patchwork of styles, ranging from Romanesque to Gothic through to Renaissance and Baroque. The basement holds a small exhibition detailing the

development of the Main Market Square over the years. Interestingly, the floor is sunk well below the level of the rest of the square, a fact that leads some to speculate the raising of the square's height at some time.

St Barbara's Church

Mały Rynek 8; free; tram: 1, 3, 6, 8; map p.133 C2

Despite the address, St Barbara's is more or less a feature of the Main Market Square as its entrance is facing that direction. Built some time during the 14th century and reputedly containing works of art inspired by if not actually made by Veit Stoss, whose masterpiece hangs in the church next door, the church's history gives a clue to the former social and ethnic strata of medieval Kraków life. Whilst neighbouring St Mary's was the church of choice for the city's elite German community, St Barbara's once served as the main church for the city's well-heeled Poles.

St Mary's Basilica

pl. Mariacki 5; tel: 12 422 0521; www.mariacki.com;

The twin towers of St Mary's Basilica were allegedly the work of two brothers. According to legend their sibling rivalry escalated to such a degree that one brother, jealous that the other was building faster and taller, murdered him. Racked with remorse, the murderer then threw himself to his death from the top of Wawel Cathedral.

Left: the spectacular interior of Wawel Cathedral *(see p.45).*

On the hour, every hour, visitors to Kraków will hear a five-note bugle call sounding from the top of St Mary's Basilica. The tune, known as the *hejnał*, cuts off abruptly, and has allegedly been played by local firemen since 1392. The call, strange as it may seem, actually honours a lone lookout who saved Kraków from Tatar invasion when he alerted the sleeping city to an enemy at the gates with his bugle call. His efforts cost him his life with a well-aimed arrow cutting short his rallying cry, cementing his actions in local legend.

Left: religious figures adorn St Adalbert's Church.

Mon–Sat 11.30am–6pm, Sun 2–6pm; admission charge; tram: 1, 3, 6, 8; map p.133 C2
Built on the foundations of a former house of worship destroyed by Tatars in the 13th century, St Mary's Basilica, a symbol of the Old Town if ever there was one, is one of the highlights of any trip to Kraków. Today's two-towered beauty owes its current external appearance to work carried out in the 14th century, although it's what's to be found inside that makes it truly special. Alive with colour and over-flowing with statues, tower-ing over everything is the extraordinary 15th-century altar of the *Quietus* by the German master Veit Stoss (Wit Stwosz), which, according to legend, took 12 years to complete. The two unequal towers, the left of which can be climbed

Right: St Mary's Basilica, lit up at night.

during the summer for breathtaking views, were said to be built by rival brothers *(see box, oppo-site)*. It's also the scene of an hourly, incomplete bugle call reputedly trumpeted over the city for hundreds of years *(see box, right)*.

OLD TOWN
Basilica of St Francis of Assisi
pl. Wszystkich Świętych 5; tel: 12 422 5376; daily 6am–8pm; free; tram: 1, 3, 6, 8;

map p.132 B1
Famously the first brick building in the city and con-secrated in the 1269 cen-tury, the interior of the gargantuan St Francis's is, unlike many churches in the city, relatively plain, with the exception of no fewer than eight jaw-dropping stained-glass windows dating from between 1895 and 1904 and designed by the city's much-lauded Stanisław Wyspiański. Of the eight, the gigantic and, at the

Left: one of the apostles on the glorious facade of St Peter and St Paul's Church.

4pm; free; tram: 3, 6, 8, 10; map p.134 C3
Overshadowed by the neighbouring St Peter and St Paul's, the Church of St Andrew's was the one church to survive the Tatar siege of 1241. The Romanesque exteriors do little to indicate the Baroque extravagances that await inside. Remodelled in 1702 by Baldassare Fontana, the interiors are a true celebration of Baroque indulgence, including a boat-shaped pulpit and 14th-century marionettes once used in Nativity plays.

Church of St Anne

ul. Św. Anny 11; tel: 12 422 5318; daily 9am–noon, 4–7pm; free; tram: 2, 3, 4, 8; map p.132 B2
Built by Tylman van Gameren in the years between 1689 and 1703, St Anne's is commonly recognised as one of the finest examples of Baroque architecture there is in Poland. Modelled in part on the Sant'Andrea della Valle in Rome, the church features the relics of St John of Kęty, dome frescoes and the intricate sculptures of Baldassare Fontana adorning the magnificent altarpiece.

Church of St Casimir

ul. Reformacka 4; tel: 12 422 2966; free; tram: 2, 3, 4, 8; map p.132 B3
This rather austere Franciscan church, built between 1666 and 1672, should be visited for two reasons. Firstly, Daniel Szulc's painting of St Casimir, regarded by art

time, controversial *God the Father in the Act of Creation* is by far the highlight. Saturday afternoons often see the church being used as a place for high-class weddings, a sight worth seeing indeed.

Bernardine Church

ul. Bernardynska 2; tel: 12 422 1650; free; tram: 3, 6, 8, 10; map p.134 C2
In 1453 Giovanni da Capistrano arrived in Kraków, and it wasn't long before his fiery speeches denouncing both wealth and Jews had won him a considerable following. The Bernardine monks he recruited built a church at the foot of Wawel, though with Swedish troops approaching it was destroyed in 1655 as part of a scorched-earth policy. Rebuilt between 1659 and

1680, the only original touches now found are the statue of the *Virgin and Child*, and some Mannerist tombs that line the wall.

Church of St Andrew the Apostle

ul. Grodzka 54; tel: 12 422 1612; daily 9am–noon, 12.30–

Legends concerning the Bernardine Church abound, although the one you're most likely to hear concerns its establishment. Back in the 14th century a light-fingered thief made off with a prized chalice from a nearby church. Pursued by a mob of angry monks, he dropped his prize on this spot, before making his empty-handed escape into the night. Guided by a mysterious, heavenly light, the monks soon located the treasured relic and decided to found the church in gratitude.

historians as one of the most influential works from 17th century Poland. Secondly, the downstairs crypt is open to the curious, and contains the naturally mummified corpses of monks and priests.

Church of St Giles
ul. Grodzka 67; free; tram: 3, 6, 8, 10; map p.134 C3
Thought to date from the 14th century, the small Church of St Giles can be identified from the Katyń Memorial Cross outside, which commemorates the Polish officers murdered by the NKVD in 1940. While a little underwhelming from the outside, the interiors of this gem are furnished in rich Baroque style, and include a crucifix from 1520 and stone stalls built in the Dutch style.

Holy Trinity Church
ul. Stolarska 12; free; tram: 1, 3, 6, 8; map p.133 C1
Currently making a name for itself as the main church used by the city's Catholic student population during evening Mass, the Holy Trinity Church was built between the 13th and 15th centuries

on the site of a former wooden church which itself was built on top of an ancient pagan temple. The Gothic red-brick exterior is a classic of its kind, and was faithfully restored after the church was seriously damaged by fire in 1850. Inside are several notable things to see, including some original bronze pieces by Veit Stoss and, at the top of the grand staircase on the left, the Rosary Chapel, complete with a famed image of *Our Lady of the Rosary*, said to have magical healing powers.

St Peter and St Paul's Church
ul. Grodzka 52a; tel: 12 422 6573; www.apostolowie.pl; Mon–Sat 7am–7pm, Sun 1.30–6pm; free; tram: 1, 3, 6, 8; map p.135 C4
The city's main Jesuit church, St Peter and St Paul's is one of the finest examples of Baroque religious architecture in the city. Famous for almost falling down soon after its construction at the start of the 17th century, the church has suffered numerous other dramas

through the centuries, including temporarily falling into the hands of the Greek Orthodox Church. Accordingly, the 12 splendid-looking Apostles over the main entrance are copies of the 18th-century originals. Among the many treasures to be found inside are the remains of the well-known Father Skarga, laid to rest inside an ornate sarcophagus in the crypt.

WAWEL
Wawel Cathedral
tel: 12 429 3327; www.wawel.krakow.pl; Mon–Sat 9am–4pm, Sun 1–4pm; admission charge for crypts and bell; tram: 3, 6, 8, 10; map p.134 B3
The third church built on this spot, Wawel Cathedral is the most important building in Poland for the country's majority Catholic population. The place where almost every Polish king and queen was crowned over the centuries, the first wooden cathedral was built soon after the founding of the Bishopric of Kraków in around 1020. The first and second churches were destroyed by fire before construction of this truly spectacular church started in the 14th century.

Consecrated in 1364 and built at the behest of the king Władysław the Elbow-High (1306–33), the first king to be crowned on the site amidst the charred remains of its predecessor, Wawel Cathedral is positively bursting with history. At its centre is the tomb of a former controversial Bishop

Left: the elaborate Corpus Christi Church *(see p.46).*

Above: the subtle exterior of the Popper Synagogue.

of Kraków, St Stanisław (1030–79), to whom the building is dedicated. There are a total of 18 chapels, all of them quite stunning, the Chapel of the Holy Cross dating from the 15th century and on the right of the main entrance being particularly impressive.

Underground, the cold and creepy Royal Crypts contain the remains of 10 kings plus the cream of the country's former heroes, including the great 19th-century Romantic poet Adam Mickiewicz, whilst at

---

Of Wawel's 10 bells, the most impressive is no doubt the 11-tonne Zygmunt's Bell. It was cast in 1520 and, reputed to be the heaviest in Poland, visitors should whisper a wish when touching its clapper, although they should also consider being well out of earshot on the rare special occasions it's rung. Anything from eight to 12 men are needed to ring this beast, with the resultant sound heard up to 50km (31 miles) away.

---

the top of a seemingly never-ending set of creaking wooden stairs is the famed Zygmunt's Bell, an 11-tonnes beast cast in 1520: it's almost compulsory to hang onto the clanger and have one's photograph taken.

KAZIMIERZ
Corpus Christi Church
ul. Bożego Ciała 26; free; tram: 3, 6, 8, 10; map p.136 C3
Completed in 1405, it's hard to miss the 70m (230ft) church tower soaring above the rest of Kazimierz. Entrance to this Gothic masterpiece is flanked by small prison cells where adulterous parishioners were once incarcerated, and the highlight is doubtlessly the breathtaking boat-shaped pulpit. Also worth investigation is the 15th-century *Madonna Terribilis Daemonibus*. The painting has been used to aid in exorcisms for the last five centuries, and is credited with warding off over 100,000 demons.

High Synagogue
ul. Józefa 38; Sun–Fri 9am–5pm; free; tram: 7, 9, 11, 13; map p.137 D4
On the ground floor of this building is a highly commended Jewish bookstore, while upstairs, you will find what remains of Kazimierz's third synagogue. Built between 1553 and 1556, this Romanesque structure was for years the highest synagogue in Kraków, with some claiming that the first-floor location was to deter Christian thugs from attacking the congregation. World War II saw the synagogue stripped of its glories, with the menorah apparently ending up as the personal loot of Nazi governor Hans Frank, and it was only after decades of neglect that funding was raised to restore the interiors. Open to the public since 2005, original details include the bare bones of the Aron Kodesh and some restored frescoes.

Isaac Synagogue
ul. Kupa 18; tel: 12 430 2222; Sun–Thur 9am–6pm, Fri 9am–2pm; admission charge; tram: 7, 9, 11, 13; map p.137 C4
Completed in 1644, construction of the Isaac Synagogue met considerable opposition from local Christians concerned it would become the most spectacular edifice in the area. They were right. Prompted by generous donations from Izaak Jakubowicz, this was to become the grandest synagogue around, for a while at least, with decorations courtesy of architects Giovanni Falconi and Giovanni Battista Trevano.

In December 1939 a Jew called Maksymilian Redlich

was shot and killed inside after refusing Nazi orders to set fire to the building, and while it was stripped and looted, it survived outright destruction. It was restored in the 1950s and temporarily used as an art commune, but since the 1990s it has housed the Centre for the Education of Jewish Youth. Today, visitors can view photographic displays and film footage covering life before and during the war.

Kupa Synagogue

ul. Midowa 27; free; tram: 3, 6, 8, 10; map p.135 E1

Also known as the Poor Synagogue, it's here that the more impoverished cross-section of Kazimierz's Jews would congregate for worship. Spurred by donations from the local community, the Kupa is thought to have been completed around 1650, and became primarily known for its vivid murals and frescoes. After the war the building was turned into a shoe factory, and it's only been in the last decade that its original glories have been painstakingly restored.

Old Synagogue

ul. Szeroka 24; tel: 12 422 0962; Tue–Sun 9am–5pm, Mon 10am–2pm; admission charge; tram: 7, 9, 11, 13; map p.137 D4

Poland's first synagogue is believed to have been erected on this site in the early 14th century, although the current structure owes much of its form to a redesign conducted by Matteo Gucci in 1570. It's alleged that Kazimierz the Great granted permission for construction of the building and even donated a pair of his personal

swords to be melted down and turned into chandeliers. Whether true or not, the tale illustrates just how important this synagogue was, and it was from on top of the *bimah* that Tadeusz Kościuszko appealed for Jews to join his 1794 uprising. In 1956 a three-year programme of restoration was undertaken, and today the synagogue hosts a fascinating museum dedicated to the history of Jewish life in Kazimierz. There's also a great bookshop upstairs in what was the women's section.

Pauline Church

ul. Skałeczna; tel: 12 421 7244; www.skalka.paulini.pl; daily 6.30am–8pm; admission charge (crypts); tram: 18, 19, 22; map p.136 A3

Known to the locals as *Skałka*, this large church by the river comes with its own special legend, namely that in 1079 King Bolesław the Bold accused the then bishop of Kraków, Stanisław Szczepański, of treasonable acts. The bishop was swiftly chopped to pieces and a curse fell upon the Polish

royal family. To appease the bishop's spirit, the Pauline Church was built. Inside is a wealth of beauty, although the church is best known for its crypt, where among others lying in eternal peace are the Lithuanian-born Nobel Prize-winning author Czesław Miłosz and the painters Stanisław Wyspiański and Jacek Malczewski.

Popper Synagogue

ul. Szeroka 16; tel: 12 421 2987; Mon–Fri 9am–2pm, 4–6pm; free; tram: 7, 9, 11, 13; map p.135 E1

Hidden behind an ivy-clad archway, it's easy to miss the Popper Synagogue, named after its founder, a wealthy merchant called Wolf Popper. Established in 1620, stewardship of the synagogue was handed to a youth culture centre in 1965, a purpose it serves to this day. The exhibitions and concerts now held here are very much worth a visit.

Remuh Synagogue

ul. Szeroka 40; tel: 12 429 5735; Sun–Fri 9am–4pm; admission charge; tram: 7, 9,

Below: the walls of the Remuh Synagogue.

11, 13; map p.135 E1
What is one of only two regularly active synagogues in Kazimierz was founded in 1553 by Rabbi Israel Isserles Auerbach. However, it's from Auerbach's son that the synagogue takes its name. Rabbi Moses Remuh achieved legendary status with his philosophies and alleged miracles, and his grave in the cemetery behind remains an important point of international pilgrimage. Pillaged by the Nazis, and used as a storeroom for body bags, the synagogue was restored in 1957 and takes in the original Aron Kodesh from 1558, as well a collection box from the

16th century. The centre-piece, the *bimah*, is a meticulous copy of the pre-war version, while the main doors are thought to hail from an unidentified syna-gogue elsewhere in Poland. Outside, to the right, is the city's oldest remaining Jewish cemetery.

Tempel Synagogue

ul. Miodowa 24; tel: 12 429 5735; Sun–Fri 10am–4pm; admission charge; tram: 3, 6, 8, 10; map p.135 D2
Constructed between 1860 and 1862, the Tempel Syn-agogue is the youngest in Kraków; its stained glass and Moorish interiors never fail to woo visitors. Striking decorations aside, it was also known for its liberal attitudes, and it was thanks to Polish- and German-language sermons, organ music and choral perform-ances that it was unoffi-cially rechristened the Progressive Synagogue. Used as a stable and store-room by the Nazis, the Tempel has since benefited from a serious amount of restoration, and there's no

better time to visit than dur-ing the Jewish Festival when its illuminated halls stage traditional klezmer concerts.

AROUND THE CENTRE
St Florian's Church

Warszawska 1b; free; tram: 2, 12, 19, 34
Originally the main Catholic church in what was once the separate town of Kleparz, St Florian's was completed in around 1216, although much of its current Baroque appearance dates from major reconstruction after a fire in the 17th cen-tury. Named after the patron saint of firefighters and, of all things, chimney sweeps, the church once marked the start of all coro-nation and royal funeral processions to Wawel. The interior is far from overly impressive but is worth a look. Perhaps of most inter-est, the late Pope John Paul II worked here when still a humble priest between 1949 and 1951. In 1999, he revisited the church and bestowed upon it the title of a lesser basilica.

As one would expect, many houses of worship in Poland don't observe strict opening times. Any fixed opening hours are noted, otherwise visitors will need to take a chance. Visiting a Catholic church dur-ing Mass is not advised, although it's possible to sneak in immediately before or after to have a look around.

Left: holy imagery at St Florian's Church.

PODGÓRZE AND PŁASZÓW

Church of the Redemptorist Fathers

ul. Zamojskiego 56; tel: 12 650 6268; free; tram: 7, 9, 11, 13

Built in neo-Romanesque form to a design by the eminent church architect Jan Sus-Zubrzycki, the Church of the Redemptorist Fathers was completed in 1906, largely thanks to the sale of 25,000 pictures of *The Mother of God of Eternal Help*. In fact, close to the wood altar visitors will find a copy of such a portrait, the one in question dating from 1865 and brought from Rome in 1903 by Father Bernard Łubieński. Also noteworthy are the elaborate stained-glass contributions of Stanisław Żeleński, as well as a series of mosaics added in the 1970s to replace inter-war polychromes.

Sanctuary of the Divine Mercy

ul. Siostry Faustyny 3; tel: 12 252 3333; daily 9am–6.30pm; free; tram: 7, 9, 11, 13

Attracting approximately two million annual visitors, this modern behemoth is Kraków's most surprising place of pilgrimage, as well as one of the city's youngest churches. Designed by Professor Edward Cęckiewicz and consecrated in 2002 by Pope John Paul II, the 5,000-capacity church features a cornerstone from Golgotha as well as a 76m

(250ft) viewing tower. However, it is for its associations with St Faustyna that the church is most famous. While attending a convent on the current church site, Sister Maria Faustyna (1905–38) started experiencing communications with God, which she transcribed in her diary. Beatified in 1993 and canonised in 2000, her relics are now on display, as well as a painting of *The Merciful Jesus*.

St Benedict's Church

ul. Rękawka; free; tram: 7, 9, 11, 13

A diminutive little church whose interiors are likely to remain as mysterious as everything else about this place, the church is believed to have been built some time in the 11th century. St Benedict's opens its doors just once a year, that being the first Tuesday after Easter to coincide with the pagan Rękawka Feast held close to the nearby Krakus Mound. Saved from demolition in the 19th century thanks to the concerted campaigning of a local priest, the single-naved St Benedict's features paintings of Benedictine friars

engaged in everyday duties as well as a Gothic vault thought to have been added in either the 15th or 16th century.

St Joseph's Church

ul. Zamojskiego 2; tel: 12 656 1756; free; tram: 1, 3, 6, 8

Dominating the local skyline is the neo-Gothic form of St Joseph's, a marvellous church completed in 1909 to a design by Jan Sus-Zubrzycki. His blueprint had originally been entered into a competition to find a design for St Saviour's in Warsaw, though it never made it past the planning stage. Marked out by an 80m (262ft) clock tower, this Podgórze showpiece features extravagant neo-Gothic sculptures added by Wit Wisz and Maksymilian Krzyk, as well as an altar crucifix clearly inspired by the work of Wit Stwosz in St Mary's. Visit during a service to hear Adolf Herman's pre-World War I organ in action.

NOWA HUTA

Arka Pana Church

ul. Obrońców Krzyża 1; tel: 12 644 5434; www.arkapana.pl; daily 6am–5pm; free; tram: 4, 16, 17, 21

Right: the Gothic structure of St Joseph's Church.

Above: the figure of Christ at Arka Pana Church.

Wojciech Pietrzyk's extraordinary design for Arka Pana was built by hand by the locals in the manner of a medieval church, between 1967 and 1977. It was the first house of worship to open in the original part of Nowa Huta. Designed to resemble Noah's Ark, the two-level building features some truly remarkable things inside, among them a controversial statue of a flying Christ, a figure of *Our Lady* *the Armoured*, fashioned from 10kg (22lb) of shrapnel from wounded Polish soldiers who fought at the infamous 1944 Battle of Monte Cassino, and a small fragment of rutile in the tabernacle brought back from the Moon by the crew of Apollo 11. Representing everything Nowa Huta was not supposed to be, the church became a popular rallying ground for early protests against the communist authorities. A highly recommended insight into the psyche of the modern Polish nation.

St Bartholomew's Church

ul. Klasztorna 11; tel: 12 644 2331; free; tram: 15, 20

Part of the Cistercian monastery complex across the street, the diminutive wooden St Bartholomew's was completed in 1466. Notable for being built in the shape of a cross and having three separate naves, the bell tower was added in the 18th century. Unfortunately, the building is almost always locked, although access can be gained if enquiries are made in St Wenceslas.

St Wenceslas Church and Cistercian Monastery

ul. Klasztorna 11; tel: 12 644 2331; free; tram: 15, 20

Work commenced on the impressive St Wenceslas Church in the mid-13th century, part of a larger ensemble that includes the adjoining Cistercian monastery and little St Bartholomew's over the road. Famous for some truly outstanding Renaissance painting inside, the church also features the bizarre *Mogiła Cross*, a figure of Christ complete with golden loincloth and real hair that supposedly grows.

KATOWICE

Christ the King Cathedral

ul. Plebiscytowa 49a; tel: 32 251 2196; Mon–Sat 6.30am–6pm, Sun 7am–6pm; free

Built between 1927 and 1955, Poland's largest cathedral is an imposing-looking neoclassical structure loved and hated in equal amounts by the locals. Victim of a change in design during construction that saw the dome shrink dramatically in size, the interior is at first glance rather dull. Closer inspection, however, reveals some gems, among them St Barbara's Chapel, dedicated to the patron saint of miners, depicting a coal-mining

Left: the Church of St Michael the Archangel.

Right: detailed decor at
St Wenceslas Church.

scene and carved from a
large piece of coal.

Church of St Michael the Archangel

ul. Gawronów 20; tel: 32 205
4061; daily 10am–4pm; free
Starting life in 1510 in the
village of Syrynia to the
southwest of Katowice, no
trip to the city's Tadeusz
Kościuszko Park is com-
plete without a visit here.
Located close to the main
road in the northwestern
part of the park, the
church was moved in 1938
and, rare for a church anywhere, is protected by a
security guard. A beautiful
little wooden structure,
inside are some fine
Gothic wooden carvings
from the 16th century.

Garrison Church of St Casimir

ul. M. Skłodowskiej-Curie 20;
tel: 32 251 3511
A fine example of inter-war
Functionalist architecture
and completed in 1933,
Katowice's only garrison
church is notable for being
one of only a handful to
boast a single corner
tower. Though sadly
locked up for much of the
time, a visit when the doors
are unlocked is rewarded
with a wealth of Art Deco
extravagance inside.

St Peter and St Paul's Church

ul. Mikołowska 32; tel: 32 251
70 45; free
Completed in 1902 using
funds donated by the
Bishop of Breslau (now the
Polish city of Wrocław),
Katowice's best example of
neo-Gothic religious architecture is a truly overpower-

ing building. Decorated
externally with some intriguing glazed green bricks
to complement the classic
red-brick style, inside are
one or two things worthy of
further investigation, among
them an original organ built
by the famous Kurzer organ
buildings from neighbouring
Gliwice and stained glass
depicting the saints to
whom the church is
dedicated. The church
served as Katowice's
cathedral until Christ the
King Cathedral was conse-
crated in 1955.

ZAKOPANE
Holy Family Church

ul. Krupówki 1a; tel: 18 201 42
47; daily 9.30am–5.30pm; free
For many visitors, the Holy
Family Church marks the
start of ul. Krupówki,
Zakopane's principal tourist
trail. Funded in part by local
bigwig Tytus Chałubiński
and designed by Warsaw's
Józef Dziekoński, this
beauty was consecrated in
1899 and deserves a visit
on account of a glorious
painted ceiling in the pres-
bytery, as well as a pair of
doors designed by the
inventor of the Zakopane
Style, Stanisław Witkiewicz.

St Mary of Częstochowa Church

ul. Kościeliska 4; daily
6.30am–7.30pm; free
Another outstanding
example of a classic
wooden parish church, St
Mary's was consecrated in
1851, although the current
structure owes much to a
complete renovation soon
after World War II. The
inside is alive with colour,
mostly in the form of traditional paintings of folk
motifs and flowers. The
adjoining cemetery is the
final resting place of many
of the town's most
respected former citizens.

Visiting churches and
synagogues in Kraków and
Poland in general requires
some respect. Short skirts
might be fine outside, but won't
be particularly welcomed in
age-old Catholic institutions.
Ditto men's legs and women's
shoulders. If entering a
synagogue, males should either
cover their heads or purchase a
skullcap *(yarmulke)*, available at
the door for a small fee. Some
churches ban photography and
are clearly signed as such. If
there's no sign, avoid using
flash, especially during Mass.

Environment

W ith its elegant parks and cobbled alleys, Kraków looks anything but an environmental black spot. The reality is, however, somewhat different. The heavy industrialisation policies adopted by the post-war communist government left a legacy of pollution, and nowhere more so than Poland's south-west. The exploitation of the steel and coal-mining industries have all contributed to heavy air pollution, and it's only recently that landmarks like Wawel have been brushed clean from the resultant factory fallout. The good news is that the city is fighting back, and concerted efforts are now underway to make Kraków greener and cleaner.

AIR POLLUTION

Kraków is, somewhat surprisingly, one of the most polluted cities in Poland and one of the few to experience problems with smog. Things have improved since communism, when there were several instances of sulphur dioxide reaching levels hazardous to the public, but there's still quite some scope for improvement.

Those playing the blame game point their finger at a number of factors. The growing number of cars clogging the streets certainly hasn't helped; neither has the fact that anything up to 30 percent of vehicles in Kraków don't comply with EU carbon dioxide rulings. Kraków's geographical position, located at the bottom of a valley, is another factor, although the chief culprit is commonly accepted to be the heavy use of coal furnaces. Since 1993 the city, boosted by EU funding, has embarked on a project to close the furnaces. So far, so good,

Above: bicycle and four-legged traffic in the city.

with the closure of 386 furnaces reducing carbon monoxide emissions by 3,706 tonnes.

Further still, considerable progress has been made in improving the public transport network to encourage people to swap the car for the tram or bus. However, the high price of gas and oil have seen a worrying increase in the use of coal. And it's not just the health of the public that stands at risk either. Scientists estimate that 1,700 historic buildings are rapidly corroding as a direct

result of polluted air. Nonetheless, if the people of Kraków have it bad, then spare a thought for the inhabitants of Zakopane, which busts myths about clean mountain air. With thousands of tourists arriving by car each day, and homes predominantly heated by coal, the smog that settles over the town sometimes reaches eight times the international air-quality standard.

RECYCLING

Kraków has embraced the concept of recycling more than any other Polish city, and huge coloured bins are evident across the town. Over 1,400 tonnes of refuse were recycled in 2008, and while the city still falls short of EU targets, the amount of recycled waste has increased by 400 percent in the last few years. An incinerator capable of coping with over half of Kraków's rubbish will soon be ready, as will plans to create 'green points' for non-biodegradable products.

Left: power-plant chimneys loom over a Kraków park.

as a 25m (82ft) tall natural stone pillar said to be the work of the devil.

THE WISŁA

The 1,047km (651-mile) Wisła (Vistula), Poland's longest river, runs the length of the country, flowing through Kraków. In recent times this age-old trading route was allowed to slip into decline, a trend only reversed by Poland's entry into the EU. A condition of entry was a wholesale clean-up by 2015, a vast undertaking set to cost 85zł billion. Cleaning the Kraków stretch is estimated at 500zł million, with projects including the creation of buffer zones and the liquidation of rubbish dumps bordering the river. Also vital to the river's revival was an overhaul of the Płaszów sewage plant, which until recently had been operated with technology dating back to the 1970s. Now, thanks in part to an EU grant to the tune of €55 million, the new-look Płaszów plant is one of the most advanced in Europe, and has cut the amount of carbon, nitrogen and phosphorus flowing into the Wisła by 97 percent.

20km (12 miles) east of Kraków, the **Puszcza Niepołomicka Nature Reserve** is an easy day trip, and features a variety of wildlife ranging from lynx to wolves. A programme to reintroduce wild bison to this former royal hunting ground has proved successful, and other attractions include 200-year-old oak and lime trees.

However, the best evidence of Kraków's new found environmental awareness can be witnessed each May. Since 2003 an annual recycling festival has been held in the Błonia park, with artists from across Poland converging to build intricate models of local landmarks out of old bottles and cans. Past artistic triumphs include a model of the Cloth Hall rendered from 60,000 bottles, and a 15m (50ft) recreation of the Florian's Gate.

WILDLIFE

Not including the city's estimated 40,000 pigeons, Kraków isn't renowned for having a diverse spread of fauna. The occasional deer, fox or weasel can be found straying into the suburbs, but chance encounters with nature aside, visitors will need to hit the national parks. The 19th-century Austrian fortresses that pepper Kraków are prime breeding grounds for bats, all of which are protected by law. Particularly endangered is the lesser horseshoe, and the snappily named Geoffroy's bat. Those wishing to catch a glimpse are advised to visit the Winnica Fort or the caves around Salonik and the Pychowicka hills.

There are a number of wildlife reserves inside the city limits, including **Las Wolski**, **Skalki Bielanskie** and **Skalki Panienskie**, although real enthusiasts should head out of town and to the **Ojców National Park**, 24km (15 miles) northwest of Kraków. Highlights in this splendid 385-hectare (950-acre) reserve include beavers, hawks and herons, as well

Below: eco-taxis in Kraków are a new initiative.

Essentials

Although generally straightforward, visiting Kraków can offer the occasional difficult moment. The advent of the low-cost airline has brought the city an increased level of Westernisation, but just like with any other culture, strangers can feel like a fish out of water. Luckily, English is now widely spoken, especially in the city centre, and hotel receptionists long ago abandoned the idea that their guests were little more than irritants to be suffered until they leave. Forging a good relationship with your hosts is always a good idea. The following provides a summary of useful information.

EMBASSIES AND CONSULATES

All of the following embassies are in Warsaw.

Australia
ul. Nowogrodzka 11; tel: 22 521 3444

New Zealand
al. Ujazdowskie 51; tel: 22 521 0500; www.nzembassy.com/poland

United Kingdom
ul. Kawalerii 12; tel: 22 311 0000; www.ukinpoland.fco.gov.uk

United States
al. Ujazdowskie 29/31; tel: 22 625 1401; http://poland.usembassy.gov

EMERGENCY NUMBERS
Fire: 998
Police: 997
Ambulance: 999

GAY AND LESBIAN
Although legal, homosexuality in conservative, Catholic Poland is something best kept discreet. Openly gay venues are few and far between, the infamous **Kitsch** club *(see Nightlife, p.99)* being one of the city's rare exceptions. For more information, take a look at www.gay.pl and click on Akceptuję Oświadczenie to state you're over 15 (the age of consent) and to reach the English pages.

HEALTH
With the exception of the brutal Kraków hangover, there are no health issues to speak of and tap water is safe to drink. However, taking out a travel insurance policy covering medical expenses is highly advisable; with the exception of private clinics, Polish medical care is far from Western standards. EU citizens possessing a European Health Insurance Card (EHIC) are entitled to cheap, occasionally free, health care.

CHEMISTS

Apteka Pod Opatrznóscia
ul. Karmelicka 23; tel: 12 631 1980; daily 24 hours; tram: 4, 8, 12, 13

A circle on a restroom door denotes ladies and a triangle means gentlemen. Most toilets are clean and come well equipped with paper.

HOSPITALS

5 Wojskowy Szpital Kliniczny
ul. Wrocławska 1–3; tel: 12 630 8324; www.5wszk.com.pl; bus: 130, 603

INTERNET ACCESS
Poland has embraced the internet like no other, and many bars, restaurants and cafés feature free wireless internet. Hotels now offer free access in their rooms as standard, with the only real exceptions being the cheapest places to stay and top-end business hotels.

Garinet
ul. Floriańska 18; tel: 12 423 2233; www.garinet.pl; daily 9am–10pm; tram: 2, 4, 7, 10
A long-standing Old Town internet café with facilities for Skype calls, printing and cheap calls abroad.

Left: police on patrol.

cheap and available widely at shops and kiosks; they are a good option for avoiding roaming charges.

TOURIST INFORMATION

The best local source of information, Kraków and the surrounding region have plenty of good tourist information points, most of them with English-speaking staff.

OLD TOWN

City Tourist Information
ul. Szpitalna 25; tel: 12 432 0110; daily 9am–7pm; tram: 2, 4, 7, 10

Małopolska Tourist Information
Rynek Główny 1/3 (Cloth Hall); tel: 12 421 7706; daily 9am–9pm; tram: 2, 4, 7, 12

KAZIMIERZ

Tourist Information
ul. Józefa 7; tel: 12 422 0471; daily 9am–5pm; tram: 7, 9, 11, 13

KATOWICE

City Information Office
ul. Rynek 13; tel: 32 259 3808; Mon–Fri 9am–6pm, Sat 9am–4pm

ZAKOPANE

Tourist Information Centre
ul. Kościuszki 17; tel: 18 201 2211; Mon–Fri 9am–5pm

LOCAL MEDIA

Kraków in Your Pocket (http://krakow.inyourpocket.com) is the best of the English-language guides, covering everything from clubs to launderettes. It is published bimonthly and is available around town for 5zł, or free in some hotels.

The dual-language *This Month in Kraków* looks and costs about the same but concentrates on the arts, including reviews of upcoming exhibitions.

The free, English-language weekly newspaper *The Kraków Post* can be found in any touristy place and is also a good source of information.

MONEY

Until 2012, when Poland is expected to join the Eurozone, the currency remains the *złoty* (zł), divided into 100 *groszy*. Although not as cheap as it was, Kraków still offers fairly good value to visitors. All major credit cards are accepted, although it's worth carrying a bit of cash around, especially outside the centre. ATMs are widespread.

POST
Main Post Office (Poczta Główna)

ul. Westerplatte 20; tel: 12 421 0348; www.poczta-polska.pl; Mon–Fri 7.30am–8.30pm, Sat 8am–2pm; tram: 1, 7, 10, 13

TELEPHONES

Poland's international dialling code is +48. To call Kraków when in Poland, note that the 12 at the start of a number is the area code and must always be included when dialling.

Pre-paid SIM cards for your mobile phone are

Left: perusing a map.

VISAS

Visitors from the EU, Australia, New Zealand, Canada and the US can visit Poland without a visa for up to three months (six months for UK passport–holders). Poland is part of the Schengen Agreement. Passports or other official ID documents with an accompanying photograph must be carried at all times.

Festivals

Validating its reputation as a world-class city, Kraków continues to grow as a destination for serious festivals and events. Every week promises something to attend, with several festivals now firmly established. Featuring everything from the hectic schedule of the highly recommended Jewish Festival of Culture to September's absurd, day-long Dachshund Parade, there's plenty to keep everyone entertained. Note that many of the city's festivals and events are movable feasts, so checking before you book your flight is advisable. For the latest information, check the Kraków Festival Office website at www.biurofestiwalowe.pl.

FEBRUARY
Shanties
www.shanties.pl
It's hard to understand why a city 600km (370 miles) from the sea should celebrate sea songs, but nevertheless, this is highly raucous and entertaining.

MARCH
Bach Days
www.amuz.krakow.pl
Organised by the city's Academy of Music, the composer is celebrated annually with a series of concerts in Florianka Hall.
SEE ALSO MUSIC, P.92

APRIL
Jazz in Kraków
www.jazz.krakow.pl
The date is as prone to improvisation at the music itself, but this festival runs for around a week at various venues around the city.

Kraków International Film Festival
www.krakowfilmfestival.pl
Celebrating its 50th anniversary in 2010, the country's most established film festival is an increasingly excellent week-long event takes place at cinemas around the city at the end of the month. Showings include everything from experimental shorts to feature films.

Soup Festival
Celebrating *barszcz*, *żurek* and other classic Polish soups, this takes place in Kazimierz's plac Nowy and boils to a conclusion with an exciting competition featuring chefs from all over the soup-drinking world.

Kraków Marathon
www.cracoviamaraton.pl
Take a picnic to the city's

Public Holidays
1 Jan: New Year's Day
Mar/Apr (varies): Easter Monday
1 May: Labour Day
3 May: Constitution Day
June (varies): Corpus Christi
15 Aug: Feast of the Assumption
1 Nov: All Saints' Day
11 Nov: Independence Day
24 Dec: Christmas Day
26 Dec: St Stephen's Day

Błonia park, where this annual event starts and finishes, for a relaxed view, or catch the athletes as they run by various city spots.

MAY
Museum Night
Visit scores of the city's best museums for just 1zł for one night of the year. Kraków's contribution is getting better all the time, with special events including the *Night of the Hassidim* in Kazimierz's Old Synagogue and some special surprises at the History of Photography Museum.

Photo Month
www.photomonth.com
Now an established part of Kraków's cultural calendar, the superb Photo Month celebrates all types of photography with a series of international exhibitions, workshops and presentations all over the city.

JUNE
Great Dragon Parade
www.groteska.pl
The mythical Wawel

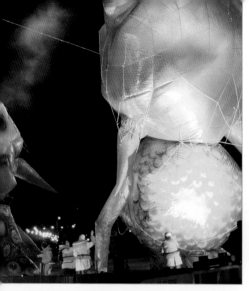

Left: the Great Dragon Parade in action.

sees ul. Floriańska and Rynek Główny transformed into one large canine cat-walk. In addition, there are sausage-dog fancy-dress and beauty competitions.

OCTOBER

Kraków Book Fair

www.targi.krakow.pl

The annual Kraków Book Fair sees the city's Targi w Krakowie conference and exhibition centre transform into a great literary cele-bration, with readings and visits from authors.

DECEMBER

Christmas Cribs Competition

The morning of the first Thursday of the month sees a presentation of the best of the year's famous Christ-mas cribs in Rynek Główny.

Christmas Market

From the end of November, Rynek Główny is trans-formed into a large market selling mulled wine, hot sausages and other treats. A stage is also built on the western side of the Cloth Hall, where a diverse series of concerts take place.

One of the strangest and loveli-est events on the annual cultural calendar is the annual New Year's Concert, held 125m (410ft) below ground in the Wieliczka Salt Mine *(see p.112)*. A highly prestigious affair, tickets get snapped up before they're printed. See www.kopalnia.pl for more information.

Dragon and his brethren from around the world are brought to life as huge pup-pets and marched around the city. It also features a number of outdoor con-certs and a spectacular firework display.

Kraków Opera Summer

www.opera.krakow.pl

Running from June to Sep-tember are a series of operas performed out-doors at the Barbican.

Wianki

Wianki (wreaths) were once worn on the heads of young maidens as part of a summer pagan festival. The event continues each 24 June next to the Wisła at the foot of Wawel Hill, where wreaths are lit with candles and floated down the river to a backdrop of live music and fireworks.

Jewish Festival of Culture

www.jewishfestival.pl

Taking place around the end of June to early July, the huge, week-long Jewish Festival of Culture breathes life back into the once vibrant ethnic community nearly wiped out in the Holocaust. It started focus-ing on intellectual seminars, but has grown into a mass event featuring everything from Jewish cookery classes to Yiddish master classes. It concludes with an amazing outdoor con-cert in ul. Szeroka.

AUGUST

Pierogi Festival

A celebration of the classic Polish dish in Mały Rynek in the Old Town and several places around Kazimierz.

SEPTEMBER

Dachshund Parade

One day each September

Below: St Mary's Basilica, lit up at Christmas.

Film

Kraków is home to April's week-long Kraków International Film Festival, one of the most respected film festivals in the country, as well as the oldest. Although the city may not be Poland's answer to Hollywood (that title goes to Łódź by a mile), cinephiles will be intrigued by Kraków's real and filmic history. In particular, the impact of Steven Spielberg's Oscar-winning blockbuster *Schindler's List*, which was based and shot in Kraków, has been key to the city's international profile. For fans of more contemporary film, the city offers many cinemas, including one with allegedly the biggest screen in Europe.

POLISH FILM

The first cinema on what's now modern Polish territory opened in 1899 in Łódź, some 250km (155 miles) north of Kraków and at the time part of the Russian Empire. The city remains the spiritual home of the Polish film industry due to its status as the country's de facto capital between 1945 and 1948, a situation that led to the opening of the infamous Łódź Film School, which never moved to Warsaw as planned and which is still in effect the country's national school of cinema. Among the school's most notable (and notorious) former students are the directors **Krzysztof Kieślowski** (1941–96), **Roman Polański** (born 1933) and **Andrzej Wajda** (born 1926), whose 1972 film *Wesele* (The Wedding) is based on the country's well-known play of the same name, written in 1901 by Stanisław Wyspiański.

Recent home-grown cinema has included Roman Polański's Oscar-winning

Above: Roman Polański.

The Pianist, released in 2002 and shot partly in Poland, *Katyń* (2007), directed by Andrzej Wajda and telling the story behind the Katyń Massacre, in which the KGB murdered 20,000 Polish officers in 1940, and David Lynch's bizarre *Inland Empire*, released in 2006 and shot mainly in Łódź.

SCHINDLER'S LIST

Although there was never much doubt Kraków would become one of Poland's most popular tourist destinations post-communism, the release of Steven Spiel-

berg's 1993 film *Schindler's List* certainly helped speed things up. Based on Thomas Keneally's 1982 book *Schindler's Ark*, the film tells the true story of Nazi Party member and businessman Oskar Schindler (1908–74), who moved to Kraków shortly after the German invasion in 1939 and opened an enamelware factory in Podgórze. The factory was staffed by Jewish employees, whom Schindler did his best to protect from the evil at work in the city, with the film following the story through to the final liquidation of Kraków's Jews and Schindler's mostly successful attempts to save his staff with the aid of the list of the film's title.

Sentimental and not entirely faithful to the book, the film is still one of immense emotion and certainly worth watching. Schindler's factory survived and is one of the many Jewish pilgrimage sites around the city. At the end of the war, Schindler fled;

Left: Spielberg directs Liam Neeson in *Schindler's List*.

A new addition to the city's cinema scene inside a former youth centre, showing a wide range of films in a small, 109-seat theatre.

Kino Pod Baranami
Rynek Główny 27; tel: 12 423 0768; www.kinopod baranami.pl; tram: 1, 3, 6, 8; map p.132 B2
Home to the annual Kraków International Film Festival among other things, this great old cinema is the best place in town to watch arthouse and underground films.

Kino Wrzos
ul. Zamoyskiego 50; tel: 12 656 1050; www.oksir.com.pl; tram: 8, 10, 11, 23
Part of a thriving centre in Podgórze; as well as a small cinema showing a wide range of films, there's a theatre, music venue, art gallery and decent café.

Orange IMAX
al. Pokoju 44; tel: 12 290 9090; www.kinoimax.pl; tram: 1, 14, 22
Allegedly the biggest screen in Europe, and the place to come for the ultimate IMAX experience.

Below: Andrzej Wajda.

The ever-increasing Polska Szkoła Dokumentu series of DVD box sets are well worth further investigation. At around 35zł for each set, which usually comes with two DVDs and an information booklet in English, the series features mostly communist-era documentaries on everything from bizarre meetings at collective farms to more personal and sometimes controversial work. Featuring the work of scores of Polish filmmakers, all of the films come with English subtitles.

Karol: A Man Who Became Pope (2005)
Pope John Paul II (2005)
Katyń (2007)
33 Scenes from Life (2008)
The Brothers Karamazov (2008)

CINEMAS
Films are usually shown in their original language with Polish subtitles. Tickets cost around 10–30zł.

ARS
ul. Św. Jana 6; tel: 12 421 4199; www.ars.pl; tram: 2, 4, 7, 12; map p.132 C3
An Old Town favourite catering predominantly but not exclusively to mainstream tastes.

Cinema City
ul. Podgórska 34; tel: 12 254 5400; www.cinema-city.pl; tram: 7, 9, 11, 13
A modern multiplex inside Galeria Kazimierz screening major Hollywood films.

Kino Agrafka
ul. Krowoderska 8; tel: 12 430 0179; www.kinoagrafka.pl; tram: 2, 3, 4, 12; map p.132 C4

as a Nazi Party member since 1930, he almost certainly would have been shot by the Red Army. After a brief spell in Argentina, he returned to Germany in 1958, four years before receiving the title Righteous Among Nations. His body lies in a Christian cemetery in Jerusalem.

KRAKÓW FILMS
The Double Life of Veronique (1991)
Schindler's List (1993)
Our God's Brother (1997)

Food and Drink

If you've ever been to Eastern Europe you'll already know many Polish dishes by sight and taste if not by name. Veritable slaves to cabbage, grilled meat, hard liquor and sweet sticky puddings, the Poles eat to live rather than live to eat, a fact that has more to do with centuries of working outdoors than anything else. Fuelled on some of the best vodka known to humanity and with their bellies bursting with artery-clogging fare, the Poles have brought their cuisine safely through the centuries almost entirely unscathed by modern influences. Forget about Michelin stars, and enjoy some hearty dishes with plenty of history.

POLISH CUISINE

MEAT DISHES

As a rule the average Pole has an almost pathological passion for meat and cabbage, and you'll find generous helpings of both applied to your dinner plate. Surprisingly, for such a nation of carnivores, the quality of steak is generally poor, with the onus instead falling on meats like chicken and pork. You'll find the ubiquitous *kotlet schabowy*, or pork chop, appearing on practically all menus, though for the seminal Polish dish order *bigos*, a sauerkraut-style stew of fermented cabbage, meat, onions, mushrooms and whatever else is found readily at hand. Considered by some to be Poland's national dish, the name *bigos* can be translated to mean 'confusion' or 'mess'.

Wild game is also popular in the higher-end restaurants, with boar, pheasant and venison all prevalent in town, although for a real local experience order the sausages. There are many types native to Poland, including the skinny *kabanos* and the pig's-blood *kaszanka*. However, in Kraków at least, the one to look for is *krakowska*, a thick sausage seasoned with pepper and garlic.

True meat-lovers, though, will look further than Kraków. The grill is

Above: traditional *pierogi*.

God in Zakopane, whose restaurants excel in the primitive pleasures of skewering animals before cooking them over open fires. The results are delicious, and very nearly worth the journey in themselves.

Golonka, a big slab of pig's thigh, is a particular favourite, although for something lighter order *gołąbki* (little pigeons), a simple dish of meat, onion and rice wrapped inside cabbage leaves. One legend attributes Poland's victory in the 1465 Battle of Malbork to a fortifying pre-combat meal of *gołąbki*.

Not unlike an oversized custard cream, the *kremówka* is a dessert of quite some pedigree. It was during his 1999 visit to Poland that Pope John Paul II confessed his love for the pudding, inadvertently prompting a sharp rocket in sales across the country. Jumping on the bandwagon, quick-thinking bakers and confectioners rebranded the tasty treat *kremówka papieska* (papal cream cake), and it's now become something of a signature snack for pilgrims in Poland. Consisting of creamy custard squeezed between two sheets of puff pastry, this dessert can be found in pretty much every bakery in town.

Left: tucking into plates of *pierogi*.

For the really weird food to come out you'll have to visit at Christmas, namely the Wigilia feast held on 24 December. Forget turkey, this is a meatless affair consisting of 12 traditional dishes that do their best to test the festive spirit. It's a highly symbolic business, with each course representing an Apostle and pride of place going to the humble carp. Purchased in the days leading up to the main event, then kept swimming in the bathtub, this bony fish is killed by the head of the household before being fried and served (bones and all) in a grey sauce to grim-faced diners.

SOUPS

There is, fortunately, more to the Polish diet than meat and meat alone. Meals usually kick off with a soup, and these encompass everything from delicious beetroot *barszcz* to *żurek*, a white rye soup sometimes embellished with sausages, potatoes and even the occasional egg floating around. Making up the third in this holy trinity of Polish soups is *flacki*, a beef tripe soup that something even the brave profess weariness towards. Be warned.

HEARTY SPECIALITIES

Far more tasty than it sounds is *smalec*, a thick chunky lard smeared onto hunks of fresh, oven-baked bread. As a winter warmer on a frosty Kraków day a helping of *smalec* can't be beaten. More evidence of the Polish affection for plain and simple food comes with *placki*, fried and fatty potato pancakes usually topped with a sour cream sauce or a mild-mannered goulash. Indeed, those hankering for anything even approaching spicy will be left disappointed by the timid nature of the Polish palate. By and large sauces are avoided, replaced instead by complements of pickled cucumbers and dill.

Pierogi, known as dumplings but really a form of ravioli, are an inescapable part of Polish cooking, and you'll find these filled with meat, cheese, cabbage and mushrooms, or even forest fruit.

PUDDINGS

Pancakes, or *naleśniki*, are another versatile mainstay, and these come with either sweet or savoury fillings. Of course, this isn't the only dessert option, and one local favourite is *makowiec*, a poppy-seed cake that always makes an appearance at Christmas. Poles are also proud of their *pączki* (doughnuts), *sernik* (cheesecake) and *faworki* (puffy, sugary pastries), and all represent a tempting way to reward your day. It's certainly a nation with a sweet tooth, and as you'd imagine, chocolate figures highly. The big local brand is Wawel, a confectionary company with a history tracing back to 1898.

Right: beetroot *barszcz*, a local favourite.

61

WHEN TO EAT

The three basic main meals eaten during the course of the day are *śniadanie* (breakfast), traditionally comprised of bread (either rye or wheat, but traditionally rye) with classic toppings in the form of ham, cheese, eggs, sausage and salad, *obiad* (lunch), which is generally a meat dish preceded with soup and often followed with a sweet, sticky desert, and *kolacja* (supper), which can be anything from a more ambitious version of breakfast to a full-blown three-course meal.

Many Poles, of course, have long since parted with tradition and will favour a more Western approach to eating, with cornflakes for *śniadanie* and a frozen pizza for *kolacja*. Other meals encountered include *drugie śniadanie* (second breakfast, or perhaps brunch) and the appetising-sounding *podwieczorek*, a light tea served between *obiad* and *śniadanie*.

ALCOHOL

VODKA

Russia or Poland? The birthplace of vodka will always divide, although no matter what side of the

The big exclusive the Kraków region has on the Polish diet is a beloved bread snack. Bagels, according to some sources, were invented by Kraków's Jewish community, apparently to celebrate King Jan Sobieski's victory over the Turks at the gates of Vienna in 1683. Surprisingly though, you'll find the bagel usurped in popularity by a far older snack, that being the pretzel-style *obwarzanek*. These have been a common sight on Kraków streets since 1394 *(see picture, left)*, with latter-day Krakovians getting through approximately 200,000 of these ring-shaped munchies every day. Priced at around 1.50zł, the *obwarzanek* is one of only two Polish regional foods protected by the EU and can be found sold from open-air stalls all over the city.

fence you sit on, there's just no disputing that Poland has utterly perfected this ancient art. There are scores of brands to look for, with the cream of the crop commonly accepted as being those from the Chopin and Belvedere factories. Luksosowa also forms part of this elite, and all three are best served ice-cold and downed in a shot. One favourite with foreigners is Zubrówka, best known for the stem of grass (from the bison fields of the east) contained in the bottle. Commonly mixed with apple juice, the brand has grown to become one of Poland's biggest exports.

For a post-feast *digestif* look no further than a gut-heating shot of *krupnik* (honey vodka) or *wiśniowka* (cherry vodka), and do also

keep an eye out for *starka*, a rye-grain vodka traditionally aged in oak barrels buried beneath the earth for up to 50 years. The practice has died out somewhat, as has Kraków's reputation for being the 'Queen of *Starka*', yet nevertheless a quick nip is as good a way as mixing with the locals as any. But before launching into a blurry binge it's wise to contemplate the habit Polish vodka has of rendering its drinkers unconscious. Falling down cellar stairwells in a drunken stupor can be easily avoided by lining the stomach during the drinking process. For the locals that usually means ordering a plate of *śledź*, or herring, a greasy yet filling accompaniment that keeps both mind and body steady.

BEER AND WINE

Despite claims to the contrary, Polish beer is generally of poor quality, with the high level of chemicals attributed to the stinging head that invariably follows a night on the tiles. Redressing the balance somewhat is the local Browar Stary Kraków brewery, whose Amber Ale can

Right: a pint of local brew.

Left: grilling *oscypek*.

Run by the Benedictine monks of the Tyniec Abbey, this little gem features cheese, jams and honey, as well as excellent beer brewed by the monks themselves.

Szambelan

ul. Gołębia 2; tel: 12 628 7093; www.szambelan.pl; Mon–Thur 10am–8pm, Fri–Sat 10am–9pm, Sun 11am–6pm; tram: 1, 3, 6, 8; map p.132 B1
Hard-to-find vodka, traditional meads and even Polish absinthe (of the non-hallucinogenic variety).

Wawel

Rynek Główny 33; tel: 12 423 1247; www.wawel.com.pl; daily 10am–7pm; tram: 2, 4, 7, 12; map p.132 B2
Find Kraków's premier confectioners doing business inside an imperial-looking building that transpires to be half shop, half café. Aside from the cakes and chocolate, look for the fudge-style *krówki*, a real Polish speciality.

compete with the best. Kraków is a city that's been hijacked by the big-money super breweries, but you can find this tipple at **Szynk** *(see Bars and Cafés, p.35)*.

Poland, and certainly Kraków, is not known for its wine, although when winter strikes do be on the lookout for *grzane wino*, mulled wine mixed with fruit and herbs. This philosophy is also applied to beer *(grzane piwo)*, and the end result makes your otherwise metallic-tasting beer endlessly palatable.

SHOPPING FOR FOOD
Kopernik

ul. Grodzka 14; tel: 12 431 1306; www.kopernik.com.pl; Mon–Fri 11am–7pm, Sat–Sun 10am–6pm; tram: 1, 3, 6, 8; map p.132 C1
The Polish city of Toruń has been producing gingerbread since the 15th century, with its contribution to confectionery culture recognised the world over. This diminutive little store allows you to see what all the fuss is about.

Krakowski Kredens

ul. Grodzka 7; tel: 12 423 8159; www.krakowskikredens.pl; Mon–Fri 10am–7pm, Sat 11am–7pm, Sun 11am–5pm; tram: 1, 3, 6, 8; map p.132 C1
Smoked hams and pots of jam fill the shelves of Krakowski Kredens, a traditional-style delicatessen which represents all that's good about the Polish kitchen. Probably the best place in town to find local specialities.

Nalewki i Inne

ul. Podgórska 34 (Galeria Kazimierz); tel: 12 433 0172; www.nalewki-i-inne.pl; Mon–Sat 10am–10pm, Sun 10am–8pm; tram: 7, 9, 11, 13
Head here for vodkas distilled and infused using an array of fruit and herbs. The gift baskets are perfect for last-minute souvenirs.

Produkty Benedyktynskie

ul. Krakowska 29; tel: 12 422 0216; www.benedicite.pl; Mon–Fri 9am–6pm, Sat 9am–2pm; tram: 3, 6, 8, 10; map p.136 B3

Whilst Kraków boasts the *obwarzanek*, Zakopane answers with *oscypek*, a tough cheese made from goat's milk and moulded into elaborate patterns. Production is taken seriously, and includes a complicated procedure that culminates in the cheese being matured in the rafters of smoke-filled huts. You won't need to look far to find a stall selling them, although do look to purchase this strange-tasting product while it's still piping hot. Fears that it would be banned under EU law for containing unpasteurised milk have proved unfounded, and it continues to be one of the best selling products from the Tatras.

History

C.50000BC
The first known human settlement appears on Wawel Hill.

1ST CENTURY AD
Kraków merchants begin trading with the Roman Empire.

965
A travelling merchant from Córdoba, Ibrahim ibn Jakub, records Kraków (Krakwa) as a thriving Slavic centre of trade.

990
The city is incorporated into the Piast dynasty, effectively bringing about the birth of the Kingdom of Poland. Soon after, the first cathedral is built.

1000
The Bishopric of Kraków is founded.

1038
The Polish capital is moved from Gniezno to Kraków.

1241
The Tatars invade Poland for the first time. As a result, Kraków's defence walls are erected.

1257
Bolesław the Chaste grants the city municipal rights. The Main Market Square is first laid out.

1335
Kazimierz is founded as a trade rival to neighbouring Kraków.

1364
The Jagiellonian University is founded as the Kraków Academy.

1410
Joint Polish and Lithuanian forces defeat the Teutonic Knights at the Battle of Grunwald, one of the greatest military battles of medieval Europe.

1494
The city's Jews are forced out of the city, settling in Kazimierz.

1596
The capital is moved to Warsaw.

1772
The First Partition of Poland.

1793
The Second Partition of Poland.

1795
The Third Partition of Poland. Kraków becomes part of Austria.

1815
The Free City of Kraków, or the Kraków Republic, is established at the Congress of Vienna.

1846
The city is absorbed into the Austro-Hungarian Empire and cultural life thrives under the relatively benign Austrian rule.

1918
Poland regains independence.

1939
Germany invades Poland on 1 September. Kraków becomes the capital of the Reich's General Government. The city's Jewish population is almost entirely wiped out during the Holocaust.

1945
A hasty German retreat leaves the city's historic centre almost intact. Poland is incorporated into the Soviet sphere of influence.

1949
Work on the first apartment blocks begins in Nowa Huta. The vast neighbouring steelworks is founded to help rebuild a country devastated by war.

1977
Work on Nowa Huta's extraordinary Arka Pana church is completed. The building becomes a focal point for the emerging anti-communist movement.

1978
Kraków's Old Town becomes the first of its kind to feature on the Unesco World Heritage list. In the same year, Karol Wojtyła, bishop of Kraków, becomes Pope John Paul II, the first non-Italian pope in over 450 years.

1981
General Wojciech Jaruzelski imposes martial law throughout Poland.

1982
Solidarity (Solidarność) is banned and its leaders imprisoned.

1983
Martial law is lifted. Solidarność's leader Lech Wałęsa receives the Nobel Peace Prize.

1989
The so-called Round Table talks produce a power-sharing agreement between the communist government and Solidarność. Wałęsa becomes the first democratically elected president of a post-communist Poland.

1999
Poland joins NATO.

2000
Kraków filmmaker Andrzej Wajda wins a lifetime achievement award at the Oscar ceremonies.

2002
In August some 2.5 million people gather in Kraków to attend Mass with Pope John Paul II.

2004
Poland joins the EU on 1 May.

2005
Pope John Paul II dies.

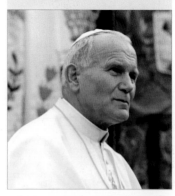

2007
Kraków celebrates its 750th anniversary.

2009
On 1 September, events take place nationwide commemorating the 70th anniversary of the German invasion of Poland and the subsequent outbreak of World War II.

Hotels

Kraków's hotels have come a long way in the last decade. Ten years ago the accommodation scene was characterised by shabby remnants of Poland's communist past and its state-run lodgings ruled with iron-fist discipline. This once dormant hotel scene exploded into life with the boom of the budget flight, and today visitors find themselves spoilt for choice. At the top end, travellers have everything from mega-brand chains to boutique hotels to pick from, whilst lower down the pecking order Kraków has an embarrassment of riches that range from family-run guesthouses to some of Europe's best hostels.

MAIN MARKET SQUARE

Hostel Rynek 7

Rynek Główny 7; tel: 12 431 1698; http://hostelrynek7.pl; €; tram: 1, 3, 6, 8; map p.132 C2

Making square-located lodging accessible to all pockets is Hostel Rynek 7, a clean, friendly venue with windows that open onto the Cloth Hall. With the exception of a couple of doubles, rooms follow the stack-a-backpacker mentality, with wood-framed bunks squeezed into long narrow rooms.

Pałac Bonerowski

ul. Św. Jana 1; tel: 12 374 1300; http://palacbonerowski.pl; €€€€; tram: 2, 4, 7, 12; map p.132 C2

Steeped in history, the Bonerwoski is a Rolls-Royce experience from start to finish, with antique decorative touches and marble bathrooms throughout. The Manggha Apartment comes clad in virgin-white colours and immaculate parquet flooring, though the real jaw-dropper is the Bonerowski Apartment. Find preserved 16th-century frescoes in one of the most luxurious rooms in Poland.

Wentzl

Rynek Główny 19; tel: 12 430 2664; http://wentzl.pl; €€€€; tram: 1, 3, 6, 8; map p.132 C2

A small, stylish hotel set over four floors of a 17th-century tenement. Decorated with hardwood floors and hand-woven rugs, most of the individually designed rooms feature windows looking out onto the square, and it's no surprise to learn of a former guest list that includes royalty. Top-floor lodgings feature a more contemporary style. DVDs and PlayStations are available from reception should Kraków fail to captivate.

OLD TOWN

Amadeus

ul. Mikołajska 20; tel: 12 429 6070; http://hotel-amadeus.pl; €€€€; tram: 2, 4, 7, 10; map p.133 D2

Open since 2000, the Amadeus is something of an old timer on the local hotel circuit, and comes with a classic design that makes use of faux-Baroque touches. The hotel lives up to its name with plenty of Viennese-style flourishes, and the formal interiors appear a favourite with the more senior traveller.

Below: outside the elegant Amadeus hotel.

Left: glossy new Kraków style at Qubus *(see p.72).*

City Hostel

ul. Św. Krzyża 21; tel: 12 426 1815; http://cityhostel.pl; €; tram: 2, 4, 7, 10; map p.133 D2

The accommodation is basic in style, with back-packers and school groups shoehorned into no-frills rooms featuring little more than beds and lockers. The real clincher here is the location, which is minutes away from both the train station and Main Market Square.

Classic

ul. Św. Tomasza 32; tel: 12 424 0303; http://hotel-classic.pl; €€€; tram: 2, 4, 7, 10; map p.133 D2

Danish-owned and designed, the Classic slots neatly into the three-star bracket. While visually unexciting, the plum-coloured rooms are kept absolutely immaculate, and the breakfast bacon is among the best in the city.

Copernicus

ul. Kanonicza 16; tel: 12 424 3400; http://hotel.com.pl; €€€€; tram: 3, 6, 8, 10; map p.134 C3

Whether it's sunset drinks on the rooftop or a wake-up swim in the cellar pool, the Copernicus is a gem from top to bottom. Merging old with new, amenities in this top-class treat include a fireplace lounge and a conference room complete with ancient scrolls, while some suites include 16th-century poly-chromes or wood-beam ceilings dating from 1370. A modern style has been adapted to fit around the historic interiors, making this legend a favourite with visiting VIPs like Prince

Paying the rack rate doesn't mean paying the best rate, and this is never truer than in Poland. The best deals on accommodation can be found via reputable web-booking agencies such as http://stay poland.com, which work in collusion with hotels to guarantee the lowest possible price. As with most net-based transactions, the earlier you book, the lower the price.

B&B La Fontaine

ul. Sławkowska 1; tel: 12 422 6564; http://bblafontaine.com; €€€; tram: 2, 4, 7, 10; map p.132 C3

Provided you've got a strong pair of legs to conquer all the stairwells, not to mention a big set of ear plugs, La Fontaine is a highly credible self-catering option. Rooms are decorated in red shades more reminiscent of the Moulin Rouge, and while the decor can't be considered snappy, you get a highly central location in return for your money.

Campanile

ul. Św. Tomasza 34; tel: 12 424 2600; http://campanile.com.pl; €€€; tram: 2, 4, 7, 10; map p.133 D2

As far as mid-range choices go the Kraków Campanile is hard to beat, and even harder when you consider the location overlooking the Planty. While this French chain offers little in the way of individuality, the hotel promises pristine, modern-looking lodgings on the edge of the Old Town action.

Below: a stately bed at the Copernicus.

Left: Pod Różą is Kraków's longest-standing hotel.

clunking old-fashioned lift, the rooms in the Saski range from standard-issue generic offerings to suites decorated in period style.

Senacki

ul. Grodzka 51; tel: 12 422 7686; http://senacki.pl; €€€; tram: 3, 6, 8, 10; map p.134 C4
What could be better than opening the curtains and seeing the magnificent St Peter and St Paul's Church outside? Grand-stand views are the Senacki's forte, although these are offset by street noise, so light sleepers should consider a room facing the courtyard. Fur-nishings are comfortable and modern, and the cross-beamed attic rooms are particularly pleasing.

Stary

ul. Szczepańska 5; tel: 12 384 0808; http://stary.hotel.com.pl; €€€€; tram: 2, 3, 4, 8; map p.132 B3
Hurt the credit card by checking into Kraków's top hotel. The pool, set inside vaulted Gothic cel-lars, looks like a Bond vil-lain's grotto, while rooms are equipped with granite sinks, Molton Brown toiletries, hardwood furnishings and traces of frescoes revealed during the renovation process.

KAZIMIERZ
Aparthotel Spatz

ul. Miodowa 11; tel: 12 424 0100; http://spatz.pl; €€€; tram: 3, 6, 8, 10; map p.135 D1
A stylish hotel with a mini-malist look that makes use of plasma screens and a combination of cream and chocolate colours. Highly

Charles and former US President George W. Bush.

Cyrano de Bergerac Apartments

ul. Sławkowska 26; tel: 508 99 7979; http://apartments-cracow-oldtown.com; €€€€; tram: 2, 4, 7, 10; map p.132 C4
Sumptuous apartments from the team behind one of Kraków's finest eateries. Touches here include a complimentary bottle of wine, a yapping dog scam-pering around and furnish-ings hand-picked from the antique stores of Europe. The Art Deco apartment is particularly becoming with Persian rugs and pre-war photos.

Gródek

ul. Na Gródku 4; tel: 12 431 9030; http://donimirski.com; €€€€; tram: 2, 4, 7, 10; map p.133 D2
It feels right to arrive at the Gródek by stagecoach, as it is a boutique effort with a Valentine spirit. Set down a secluded cul-de-sac, it has the style of a country mansion, accentuated by comfortable rooms with plump pillows and antique-style fittings.

Pod Różą

ul. Floriańska 14; tel: 12 424 3300; http://hotel.com.pl; €€€€; tram: 2, 4, 7, 10; map p.133 C3
Kraków's oldest hotel has quite some guestbook. Tsar Alexander I once bunked here, and he was followed by Honoré de Balzac and Napoleon's Persian emissary. Today, the boutique design has heavy shades of the past, with details such as 19th-century tiled stoves and restored frescoes appear-ing in some of the rooms.

Saski

ul. Sławkowska 3; tel: 12 421 4222; http://hotelsaski.com.pl; €€; tram: 2, 4, 7, 10; map p.132 C3
This venerable establish-ment comes with a rich history, with Franz Liszt and the Brahms brothers once headlining in the ball-room. Accessed via a

Price ranges, given as a guide only, for a standard double room in peak season:
€€€€ over 500zł
€€€ 300–500zł
€€ 150–300zł
€ under 150zł

recommended, though at this price you may expect a greater range of facilities, such as maid service and air-conditioning.

Astoria
ul. Józefa 24; tel: 12 432 5010; http://astoriahotel.pl; €€; tram: 7, 9, 11, 13; map p.135 E1
A spotless three-star jaunt with a fuchsia facade and rooms decorated in pink and brown. While the rather neutral design won't stir you to flights of fancy, the welcome at the front desk is warm and the location bang in the centre of Kazimierz.

Eden
ul. Ciemna 15; tel: 12 430 6565; http://hoteleden.pl; €€; tram: 7, 9, 11, 13; map p.135 E1
What was once the abode of Izaak Jakubowicz, founder of the nearby synagogue, now plies its trade as a rather middling hotel. Some rooms require an update, though on the whole you will find value for money inside a pleasant space that touts a *mikveh* bath and the only kosher restaurant in the city.

Karmel
ul. Kupa 15; tel: 12 430 6700; http://karmel.com.pl; €€€; tram: 7, 9, 11, 13; map p.135 E1
Lugging your luggage upstairs isn't much fun, and the rooms are a bit of a squash, but negatives aside, the Karmel is a bit of a treasure, with well-appointed quarters, ice-cream-white designs and a side-street location on one of the area's quieter thoroughfares.

Kazimierz's Secret
ul. Józefa 34; tel: 12 428 0115; http://kazimierzs-secret.com; €€; tram: 7, 9, 11, 13; map p.135 D1
Ten-plus apartments, all recently completed to a high standard. With names like Bishop's Apartment and Lucky Number 13 the digs are nowhere near as imaginative as one envisages, but offer good-quality comfort as well as everything from washing machines to kitchens.

Klezmer Hois
ul. Szeroka 6; tel: 12 411 1245; http://klezmer.pl; €€; tram: 7, 9, 11, 13; map p.135 E2
So what if some of the rooms are starting to look

Top-range hotels will often attract the attention of unlicensed cab drivers, so avoid rip-offs by making sure any taxi you use is clearly marked with its rates displayed on the window. Also be aware that some of the better-class hotels use their own official taxis, which will also often charge well above and beyond the going rate. Nasty surprises can be avoided by arranging a fee beforehand, or asking reception to call a reputable company (see also Transport, p.125).

a little stained and frayed, there's no denying Klezmer Hois has charisma by the bucket. Set at the top of ul. Szeroka, a stay in KH is like peering into another era. Filled with squeaking floors and wrought-iron beds, this isn't so much a hotel as a trip back in time.

Kolory Bed and Breakfast
ul. Estery 10; tel: 12 421 0465; http://kolory.com.pl; €; tram: 7, 9, 11, 13; map p.135 E1
A superb budget option set right above a craft store. Painted puppets, clay cats and little

Below left: the Karmel. **Below right:** the dining room at the Rubinstein *(see p.70).*

Left: the Tournet is basic but brilliantly located.

AROUND THE CENTRE

Andel's

ul. Pawia 3; tel: 12 660 0000; http://andelscracow.com; €€€€; tram: 2, 4, 7, 10; map p.133 E4

Designed by Jestico & Whiles, the Andel's takes the appearance of a glass and granite cube, and its ultra-modern interiors include flat-screen televisions, DVD players, floor-to-ceiling windows and walk-in showers lit by strips of neon.

Benefis

ul. Barska 2; tel: 12 252 0710; http://hotelbenefis.pl; €€€; tram: 18, 19, 22

Benefis is the very definition of three-star, and while the onus is on functionality, the rooms are smart, sharp and brightened with whimsical touches like leaf-patterned duvets and dashes of modern art.

Dom Turysty

ul. Marii Curie Skłodowskiej 6; tel. 012 421 4444; http://dom turysty.info; €; tram: 7, 10, 13; map p.133 E2

Some backpackers criticise the lack of atmosphere in this spot, which translates to mean that there's more chance of sleep and less chance of parties. A more learned censure would be the amount of steps travellers must climb, though even accounting for that this is a cracking deal, touting steel frame beds, a neat look and televisions.

Etap

al. Armii Krajowej 11a; tel: 12 626 1145; http://accorhotels. com; €€; tram: 14, 24

cherubs embellish the whitewashed walls, with plenty more folksy charm added by way of embroidered cushions, lace and frills.

Rubinstein

ul. Szeroka 12; tel: 12 384 0000; http://hotelrubinstein.com; €€€€; tram: 7, 9, 11, 13; map p.135 E1

Almost all hotels of note include breakfast in the price of the room, with a few charging extra and the absolute minority offering no breakfast at all. Hotel breakfast in Poland can mean anything from a choice of traditional communist-style leathery omelettes from a limited menu to a slap-up smorgasbord in the city's five-star establishments. Those who believe breakfast to be the most important meal of the day are advised to check what's on offer before booking a room.

Named after the Queen of Cosmetics, who was born next door, the Rubinstein is an outstanding deal with a vaulted entrance hall, wood-beamed ceilings and the classy atmosphere of days of yore. A particular favourite is the Column Suite, featuring 16th-century pillars and furniture garnered exclusively from the 18th and 19th centuries.

Tournet

ul. Miodowa 7; tel: 12 292 0088; http://accommodation. krakow.pl; €; tram: 3, 6, 8, 10; map p.135 D1

A cheap and cheerful guesthouse with simple rooms themed by colour and equipped with little more than televisions, beds and a separate bathroom. What you get is an excellent location and plenty of change left over to spend in the hostelries around.

A clean, modern hotel with a no-frills design and an awkward positioning that will leave you well acquainted with taxis and trams. Functional rooms come in clinical colours, and while the identikit style is little to enthuse about, the price-to-value ratio is simply unbeatable.

Giraffe

ul. Krowoderska 31; tel: 5092 594 66; http://hostelgiraffe.com; €; tram: 3, 7
Part of the new generation of hostels that has sprung up during over the last few years, the Giraffe is best enjoyed if you're under a certain age (say 25). As the free check-in beer suggests, drunkenness is rife and encouraged, with the drinking not always limited to the bar area. As fastidiously clean as a hostel environment allows, perks at the Giraffe include laundry, lockers and linen, with dorms and showers furnished to a modern standard.

Greg & Tom Hostel

ul. Pawia 12/7; tel: 12 422 4100; http://gregtomhostel.com; €; tram: 2, 4, 7, 10; map p.133 E4
Stags and school groups are banned by Greg & Tom, and with dorms housing no more than six people it's odds on for a solid night's sleep. There's a real atmosphere of intimacy here, and with six computers to share between a maximum of 23 guests there are no queues while waiting for a homesick Australian to finish a Skype call.

Holiday Inn

ul. Wielopole 4; tel: 12 619 0000; http://hik.krakow.pl; €€€€; tram: 1, 7, 10, 13; map p.133 D1
While lacking the cutting edge design dazzle of Kraków's newer five-stars, the Holiday Inn remains a wise and popular choice. Amply proportioned rooms come with luxurious beds, soundproofed windows and a reserved style that while uneventful is pleasant enough. Breakfast, regrettably conducted in a windowless basement, gets full marks, while the location is just steps away from the Planty.

Nathan's Villa Hostel

ul. Św. Agnieszki 1; tel: 12 422 3545; http://nathansvilla.com; €; tram: 3, 6, 8, 10; map p.135 C1
The first hostel to do away with curfews and kick-out times, no other place has done more to put Kraków on the backpacking map. Primarily known as a party place, you'll find a bar downstairs and in it quite probably Nathan himself, leading his guests astray. There is a choice of well-kept private rooms, while more cash-conscious travellers make do with prim-looking dorms equipped with fat mattresses.

Patac Pugetów

ul. Starowiślna 15a; tel: 12 432 4950; http://donimirski.com; €€€; tram: 1, 7, 10, 13; map p.135 D4
A honeymoon experience set in a restored mansion house, the Pugetów is adorned with portraits of 19th-century damsels. Rooms in this romantic hideaway include fluffy bathrobes and locally sourced toiletries. While lacking in lifts and other extras, Pugetów redeems itself with oodles of character and obliging staff.

Radisson SAS

ul. Straszewskiego 17; tel: 12 618 8888; http://radissonsas.com; €€€€; tram: 2, 3, 4, 8; map p.132 A1
What else to expect from the Radisson but chic, five-star style? Overlooking the Planty, it also offers a brunch buffet that's renowned across town, and unlike others in its bracket, free internet throughout.

Below: the ultra-modern Andel's.

Red Brick Apartments

ul. Kurniki 3; tel: 12 628 6600; http://redbrick.pl; €€€; tram: 12, 19; map p.133 D4

Fantastic value inside a restored brick building originally completed in 1893. Apartments come with fully fitted kitchens, giant LCD screens and soft and soothing brown colours that are far nicer than they sound. Sleeping anything from one to six people, particular praise goes to the de luxe option, complete with a corner balcony.

Sheraton Krakow

ul. Powiśle 7; tel: 12 662 1000; http://sheraton.com/krakow;

Price ranges, given as a guide only, for a standard double room in peak season:
€€€€ over 500zł
€€€   300–500zł
€€   150–300zł
€   under 150zł

€€€€; tram: 1, 2, 6; map p.134 A3

All the luxury in the world comes packed and parcelled beneath a breathtaking glass roof. This is every bit the top-drawer experience one expects from the Sheraton brand, and it's unlikely you'll find a better bed in Kraków.

PODGÓRZE AND PŁASZÓW

Qubus

ul. Nadwiślańska 6; tel: 12 374 5100; http://qubushotel.com; €€€; tram: 7, 9, 11, 13; map p.137 E2

A curvy looking building with a glass-covered atrium and swish rooms decorated with polished woods and vanilla splashes. Qubus might be on the wrong side of the river, but there's no doubting this is one of the better deals in town, particularly for those with a business agenda.

NOWA HUTA

JB Hotel

ul. Ujastek Mogilski 7; tel: 12 680 7100; http://hoteljb.com.pl; €€; tram: 15, 17, 21

If, by some unforeseen circumstance, you find yourself staying in Nowa Huta, then the JB offers a fabulous alternative to the communist relics it competes with. Set in the sort of glass building you'd expect in a retail park, this hotel comes with uniform blue rooms and a covered conservatory that is open all year round.

Santorini

ul. Bulwarowa 35b; tel: 12 680 5195; http://santorini.krakow.pl; €€; tram: 5

Avoid the lads and stags who land in Kraków each weekend by staying in Nowa Huta. Built in 2006, the Santorini (Greek-themed restaurant downstairs, hence the name),

Left: chic design at the Radisson SAS *(see p.71)*.

has quiet rooms and a simple, homely style making use of muted browns.

KATOWICE
Diament
ul. Dworcowa 9; tel: 32 253 9041; http://hoteldiament.pl; €€
Characterised by large, peach-coloured rooms, the Diament might not be as classy as the neighbouring Monopol, but that hasn't stopped a few famous faces from swinging by (photographic proof in the lobby). Katowice's best source of mid-range accommodation is just minutes from the train station and run by a local chain with hotels spread around Silesia.

Monopol
ul. Dworcowa 5; tel: 32 782 8282; http://hotel.com.pl; €€€€
A creepy looking neo-Gothic facade hides a de luxe spot which mixes industrial touches (exposed pipes, pictures of collieries) with fanciful Art Deco flourishes that run from walnut fittings to the occasional safari trophy. Bedrooms come appointed with inter-war furnishings and are simply the best you'll find in the city.

Olimpijski
al. Korfantego 35; tel: 32 258 2282; http://hotelspodek. katowice.pl; €
Pretend you've been kidnapped by aliens by staying in the Spodek, Katowice's very own UFO-shaped building. The lobby is all rubber plants and marble cladding,

while a series of curving corridors lead guests past plastic Greek pillars to budget accommodation kitted out with the sort of furniture you'd usually find in an office.

ZAKOPANE
Grand Hotel Starmary
ul. Kościuszki 19; tel: 18 202 4510; http://stamary.pl; €€€
Eclipsing Zakopane's other hotels, the Starmary adds a touch of class to a town saturated with on-the-cheap options. Set in a steep-roofed, stone and brick villa, this place has a country club look, an excellent spa and rooms decorated in plush tones.

Gubałówka
ul. Zubka 4; tel: 18 206 2795; http://gubalowka.pl; €
Here's the ultimate refuge from the noise and neon of Krupówki. Found at the top of the funicular railway the Gubałówka offers unrivalled views of the Tatras as well as accommodation inside a chalet building rendered from

> Whereas some countries favour leaving a copy of the Bible in hotel rooms, Poland's particular penchant is for bottled mineral water. Many hotels not only leave small bottles of complimentary water for their guests but even replace them daily. Unless the bottle is clearly marked with a price, feel free to drink at your leisure.

pine. Rooms are kitted out with little more than beds and bathrooms, but the simple wood-finished design is tidy and tasteful.

Sabała
ul. Krupówki 11; tel: 18 201 5092; http://sabala. zakopane.pl; €€
A giant chalet planted on Zakopane's busiest street, rooms come with log-cutter furnishings and warming winter extras such as heated bathroom flooring, while the sauna and pool are among the best in town. Noise from the live mountain bands who lurk the streets can be a problem.

Below: the highly recommended Monopol.

Language

Polish, a Slavic language, has a complex grammar and can be difficult to pronounce with its long sequences of consonants, but it has the advantage of being pronounced exactly the way it's spelt. Some regions of Poland are very attached to their dialects, such as *Góralski*, spoken in the Podhale district, *Kashubian*, used by an ethnic minority in Pomerania, and *Silesian*, the language of southwestern Poles. However, standard Polish is spoken everywhere by everyone. In larger Polish cities, you won't have trouble communicating in English, and efforts have been made in recent years to translate signs and menus for English-speaking visitors.

GENERAL

Yes *Tak*
No *Nie*
Please *Proszę*
Thank you *Dziękuję*
Excuse me *Przepraszam*
You're welcome *Proszę*
Hello/Hi *Dzień dobry/ Cześć (informal)*
Goodbye *Dowidzenia/ Cześć (informal)*
Do you speak English? *Czy mówisz po angielsku?*
I don't understand *Nie rozumiem*
I'm sorry *Przepraszam*
I don't know *Nie wiem*
My name is... *Mam na imię...*

Nice to meet you
Miło poznać
What is your name? *Jak masz na imię?*
I am English/American *Jestem z Anglii/z Ameryki*
When? *Kiedy?*
At what time? *O której?*
today *dzisiaj*
yesterday *wczoraj*
tomorrow *jutro*
now/later *teraz/później*
morning *rano*
afternoon *popołudnie*
evening *wieczór*
day/week *dzień/tydzień*
month/year *miesiąc/rok*
left *lewo*
right *prawo*

ON ARRIVAL

Where is there a bus/ tram stop? *Gdzie jest przystanek autobusowy/ tramwajowy?*
railway station *dworzec kolejowy*
airport *lotnisko*
cab rank *postój taksówek*
one-way ticket *bilet w jedną stronę*
return ticket *bilet w dwie strony*
I'd like a single/ double room *Poproszę pokój jednoosobowy/ dwuosobowy*
What is the charge per night? *Ile kosztuje doba?*

EMERGENCIES

Help! *Pomocy!*
Call a doctor/an ambulance *Proszę wezwać lekarza/karetkę*
Call the police/fire brigade *Proszę wezwać policję/straż pożarną*
Where's the nearest hospital? *Gdzie jest najbliższy szpital?*
I am sick *Jestem chory(a)**

Left: Polish editions of popular magazines.

Left: using a few Polish words is always appreciated.

wegetarianką
I'd like to order *Chciał(a)bym zamówić*
Enjoy your meal! *Smacznego!*
tip *napiwek*
smoking/non-smoking *dla palących/ dla niepalących*

DAYS OF THE WEEK
Monday *poniedziałek*
Tuesday *wtorek*
Wednesday *środa*
Thursday *czwartek*
Friday *piątek*
Saturday *sobota*
Sunday *niedziela*

NUMBERS
0 *zero*
1 *jeden*
2 *dwa*
3 *trzy*
4 *cztery*
5 *pięć*
6 *sześć*
7 *siedem*
8 *osiem*
9 *dziewięć*
10 *dziesięć*
11 *jedenaście*
12 *dwanaście*
13 *trzynaście*
14 *czternaście*
15 *piętnaście*
16 *szesnaście*
17 *siedemnaście*
18 *osiemnaście*
19 *dziewiętnaście*
20 *dwadzieścia*
30 *trzydzieści*
40 *czterdzieści*
50 *pięćdziesiąt*
60 *sześćdziesiąt*
70 *siedemdziesiąt*
80 *osiemdziesiąt*
90 *dziewięćdziesiąt*
100 *sto*
1000 *tysiąc*

These letters are pronounced:
ą like 'on' in wrong
c like 'ts' in bits
ć, cz, ci like 'ch'
ch like 'h'
ę like 'en' in penguin
g like 'g' in goat
j like 'y' in yet
ł like 'w' in wet
ń, ni like 'ni' in Narnia
ó like 'oo' in pool
rz like 'si' in vision
ś, sz, si like 'sh' in shine
w like 'v' in vat
y like 'i' in pig
ż, ź, zi like 'si' in vision

I have lost my money/passport/luggage *Zgubiłem(am) pieniądze/ passport/bagaż*
pharmacy/chemists *apteka*

SHOPPING
How much is it? *Ile to kosztuje?*
Have you got...? *Czy ma Pani/Pan...?*
enough *wystarczy*
too much *za dużo*
a piece *kawałek*
each *każdy*
Do you take credit cards? *Czy można płacić kartą?*
Is there a bank/ATM near here? *Czy jest w pobliżu bank/bankomat?*
shopping mall *centrum handlowe*
market *rynek*
supermarket *supermarket*
postcard *pocztówka*
stamp *znaczek*
open/closed *otwarte/ zamknięte*

SIGHTSEEING
Where is...? *Gdzie jest...?*
tourist information office *informacja turystyczna*
church *kościół*
exhibition *wystawa*
museum *museum*
guide *przewodnik*
free *za darmo*

DINING OUT
breakfast *śniadanie*
lunch *lunch/obiad*
dinner *kolacja*
meal *posiłek*
first course *pierwsze danie*
main course *drugie danie*
the bill *rachunek*
I am a vegetarian *Jestem wegetarianinem/*

Note: 'a' is the feminine ending for adjectives, nouns and verbs.

75

Literature

Poland has a long and proud literary tradition that stretches back to medieval times when scribes like Jan Długosz (1415–80) chronicled the events of the era. In the following centuries, Polish talents such as the Romantic poet Adam Mickiewicz (1798–1855) and the Nobel Prize-winning author Henryk Sienkiewicz (1846–1916) came to the fore, blending Romanticism with patriotism during a time of Tsarist hegemony. As Poland's self-declared cultural capital, it should come as no surprise that Kraków too has made an impact on the literary world, and it's contribution to national literature can't be underestimated.

KRAKÓW WRITERS

With over 27 million copies sold, and works translated into over 40 languages, science fiction writer and former Jagiellonian University medical student **Stanisław Lem** (1921–2006) stands out as one of Poland's best-known authors, with his seminal work *Solaris* twice made into film.

Lithuanian born **Czesław Miłosz** (1911–2004) is popularly considered as Poland's finest writer of the 20th century, and his 1953 defining masterpiece, *The Captive Mind*, is a fascinating study of the human psyche. Miłosz was awarded the Nobel Prize for Literature in 1980 and spent much of his time in Kraków both before and after the fall of the Iron Curtain. He lies buried in the city's Pauline Church.

Kraków-based **Wisława Szymborska** (b.1923) is one of Poland's greatest living poets, and despite penning fewer than 250 poems, is a well-known figure who won international recognition when she was awarded the Nobel Prize for Literature in 1996.

Stanisław Ignacy Witkiewicz (1885–1939), also known as Witkacy, was one of the great avant-garde figures of inter-war Poland. Heavily influenced by drugs and depression, works of this multi-talented eccentric include plays and paintings, as well as novels such as *The Madman and the Nun* and *The Crazy Locomotive*. He committed suicide on the day of the Soviet invasion, and now lies buried in Zakopane, a town in which he spent much of his life.

HOLOCAUST LITERATURE

Kraków's proximity to Auschwitz, the dark heart of the Holocaust, means there's no shortage of books, dissertations and guides covering the tragic events that unfolded there. The best-known work of all, and the key reason Kraków found itself exposed to mass tourism in the first

Above: Stanisław Lem.

place, is **Thomas Keneally's** excellent 1982 *Schindler's Ark*, later made into the Oscar-winning *Schindler's List* by director Steven Spielberg *(see Film, p.58)*. Set in Schindler's Podgórze factory and the nearby Płaszów labour camp, Keneally's novel paints a vivid picture of wartime Kraków.

Primo Levi (1919–87), the Italian chemist and Holocaust survivor, however, penned the seminal Auschwitz work. *If This is a Man* tells his story, with detached prose picking up the minutiae and describing

Left: browsing at Massolit.

11am–7pm; tram: 1, 3, 6, 8, 18; map p.133 D2

Great big coffee-table books on sale with titles focusing on a broad choice of topics. While there are quite a few Polish titles worth investigating (photography, architecture), the spotlight is by and large more concerned with the works of Western photographers, with prices similar to what you'd find at home.

Jarden

ul. Szeroka 2; tel: 12 429 1374; www.jarden.pl; Mon–Fri 9am–6pm, Sat–Sun 10am–6pm; tram: 7, 9, 11, 13; map p.135 E2

Over 500 titles, including cookbooks, Kraków tours, history and Holocaust. Books in languages including English, German, French and Yiddish are available, as are collectors' items, plus a staff who go beyond the call of duty when it comes to locating that hard-to-find title the customer is chasing.

Massolit

ul. Felicjanek 4; tel: 12 432 4150; www.massolit.com; Sun–Thur 10am–8pm, Fri–Sat 10am–9pm; tram: 1, 3, 6, 8; map p.134 A4

Named after the black cat in Bulgakov's *The Master and Margarita*, this is your classic second-hand bookshop, complete with expats huddled over coffee and cakes. Books cover a multitude of obscure subjects, and the rarer the title, the more chance you have of finding it. Those wishing to make Kraków home should check the notice board, chock-full of Post-It notes appealing for flats and language teachers.

---

in detail the dehumanisation process experienced by inmates. If you wish to read one Holocaust-themed book, make it this one.

The Polish poet and academic **Tadeusz Borowski** (1922–51) also warrants investigation for his classic *This Way For the Gas, Ladies and Gentlemen*. Written with a fine eye for detail, Borowski describes his incarceration in Auschwitz, in a chilling story of daily survival.

Meanwhile, **Sybille Steinbacher's** recent *Auschwitz* provides a fine historical overview, with the author displaying considerable skill in unearthing hitherto unknown facts.

BOOKSHOPS
American Bookstore

ul. Pawia 5 (Galeria Krakowska); tel: 12 628 7573; www.american bookstore.pl; Mon–Sat 9am–10pm, Sun 10am–9pm; tram: 7, 9, 11, 13; map p.133 E4

The AB excels in importing best-selling titles. A good place to pick up some unchallenging reading.

EMPiK

Rynek Główny 5; tel: 12 429 4162; www.empik.com; daily 9am–10pm; tram: 1, 3, 6, 8, 18; map p.132 C2

A Polish mega-chain with a decent section set aside for English-language press (usually a few days out of date) as well as an interesting mix of trash fiction, classics and a few audio books. Maps and guides are also available.

House of Albums

ul. Św. Tomasza 25; tel: 12 429 1363; www.houseofalbums.pl; Mon–Fri 10am–7pm, Sat–Sun

---

Translated into English and written by locals with an excellent in-depth knowledge of their subjects, Agnieszka Legutko-Ołownia's *Kraków's Kazimierz* and Maciej Miezian's *Kraków's Nowa Huta* and *Kraków's Old Town* are more than worth the 35zł or so cover price. Full of bizarre facts, suggested walks and valuable insights, the illustrated, pocket-sized guides are available in several bookshops around the city.

Markets

From the rows of tourist trinkets laid out inside and around the Cloth Hall to the olfactory-challenging whiff of sausages for sale at Stary Kleparz, exploring the city's manifold markets is one of the great pleasures of a visit to Kraków at any time of year. Tourist traps aside, the classic Eastern European market is alive and well in Poland and continues to feed and clothe a nation of shoppers still not entirely won over by the ever-encroaching out-of-town shopping centres. Whether you go to shop or just to soak up the atmosphere, the following listings suggest the best of the bunch to visit.

MAIN MARKET SQUARE
Cloth Hall

Rynek Główny; Mon–Fri 10am–7pm, Sat–Sun 1am–6pm; tram: 2, 4, 7, 12; map p.132 C2
Originally just two walls between which traders would store their goods for the night, embellishments were added throughout the 13th century, until finally, the fol-lowing century, Kazimierz the Great decreed the complex be covered. Reconstructed several times over the centuries, the wedding cake-looking Cloth Hall of today is still an important trading point and a must-visit for sou-venir hunters. Flanked with stalls selling craftwork, jewellery, pottery, paintings and amber, this colon-naded building offers the ultimate solution to last-minute gift emergencies.

Each December the Main Market Square plays host to the annual Christmas Market, filling with wooden huts selling mulled wine, honey, handicrafts and mountain cheese. It's a scene that wouldn't be out of place in Dicken's *A Christmas Carol*, and pride of place goes to the exhibi-tion of Christmas cribs next to the Adam Mickiewicz Monu-ment. Exceedingly ornate mod-els of Nativity scenes and local churches are laid out on display before being judged to deter-mine the winning entry. The best designs find themselves inducted into a special exhibition inside the Kraków History Museum. *See also Festivals, p.57; Monuments, p.80.*

Flower Market

Rynek Główny; daily 6am–10pm; tram: 2, 4, 7, 12; map p.132 C2
One of the enduring tradi-tions of the Main Market Square is the flower mar-ket that stands between St Mary's Basilica and the Cloth Hall. Operating since the beginning of the 16th century, the market is staffed exclusively by women, with many of the stalls handed down from generation to generation. Operating long into the night, it's the local custom

Above: fresh fruit for sale.

for these hardy traders to bestow flowers on visiting dignitaries, as well as to hand out mistletoe to the public on Christmas Eve.

KAZIMIERZ
Kazimierz Market

pl. Nowy; daily 5.30am–3pm; tram: 7, 9, 11, 13; map p.135 D1
A red-brick rotunda forms the centrepiece of the Kaz-imierz market, and it's here you'll find Kraków's only horsemeat on sale. Once operating a Jewish slaugh-terhouse for poultry, the building today houses a couple of local deli-catessens as well as a

Left: be sure to visit bustling Cloth Hall.

in slightly less than salubrious surroundings, nightfall hereabouts heralds several local ladies of the night.

ZAKOPANE

One could be excused for thinking that Zakopane's streets are, during the high summer season at least, one big outdoor market. From the moment you step off the bus, pavements positively bulge with traders selling everything from recommended local food produce to ghastly plastic mementoes of your stay. However, those who pride themselves on sorting the wheat from the chaff will be rewarded with some real treats. The two best (and worst) places to explore are the length of ul. Krupówki, where some surprisingly good bargains can be picked up if you're prepared to haggle, and, at the street's far end, the large outdoor market next to the funicular railway. Daytime activity here sees the locals setting up shop and selling everything from wooden toys to artificial sheepskin rugs to CDs of the sort of folk music played in every other restaurant in town.

number of fast-food outlets. However, head to the market's perimeters for the main action, with traders operating from the crack of dawn, selling everything from fake designer handbags and sheepskin coats to pre-war treasures recovered from the attic. Visit on Tuesdays to witness the vaguely depressing domestic pet market, or on Thursday for the equally alarming pigeon fair.

AROUND THE CENTRE
Hala Targowa
pl. Targowy; Mon–Sat 6am–7pm, Sun 6am–2pm; tram: 1, 11, 14, 22
Ignore the indoor supermarket and explore the outdoor section to the right. A classic Eastern European experience, here you can rub shoulders with everybody from students to grannies fighting over rows of bargains featuring everything from local dried mushrooms to imported Chinese tat to dubious DVDs. Watch your wallets at all times and remember that in many cases haggling here is considered fair game.

Stary Kleparz
Rynek Kleparski; Mon–Sat 6am–6pm; tram: 2, 4, 5, 12; map p.133 D4
One of the city's oldest markets, this cramped outdoor attraction is worth a look around. Refreshingly tourist-free, this is one of the best places in the city for fresh food, including fruit, vegetables, magnificent smoked sausages and local cheese. Located

Right: buy mountain cheese in Zakopane.

79

Monuments

A city's monuments more often than not conceal fascinating stories that help unlock the character of a destination, especially in a city with as dramatic a history as Kraków. Its fine collection of monuments, statues and cemeteries, of which the mere tip of the iceberg is mentioned here, provides enough information to fill a book twice over, all of it free to visit and available 24 hours a day. Brushing shoulders with the city's monumental heavyweights celebrating national heroes and moments of immense historical pride are a few modern masterpieces and the occasionally eccentric, typically Polish, sight.

ADAM MICKIEWICZ MONUMENT
Rynek Główny; tram: 2, 4, 7, 12; map p.132 C2

The late, great, Lithuanian-born Romantic poet Adam Mickiewicz (1798–1855) is immortalised in the centre of the Old Town courtesy of this 1955 copy of the 1898 original by Teodor Rygier. Destroyed by the occupying Germans during World War II, the elaborate monument is considered to be one of the most important statues in the country and is now a popular meeting place. Adam Mickiewicz, who never visited Kraków, is buried just down the road in Wawel Cathedral.

EROS BENDATO
Rynek Główny; tram: 2, 4, 7, 12; map p.132 B2

The German-born Polish contemporary artist Igor Mitoraj's decidedly modern-looking head on its side swathed in bandages is a welcome addition to the square's predominantly antiquated sights. Part of a huge series of

Above: a detail of the Ghetto Heroes' Square memorial.

similar works that all feature a bandage theme, many with broken limbs representing the classic statues of ancient Greece, Mitoraj's Old Town classic has been designed so that people can climb around inside, making it a popular place for holiday snaps.

GHETTO HEROES' SQUARE
plac Bohaterów Getta; tram: 7, 9, 11, 13; map p.137 E2

This large open space of grey concrete just south of the river has been trans-formed into a beguiling and moving work of art com-memorating the terrible events in 1943 when the Ghetto was finally liqui-dated. Comprising some 70 bronze chairs scattered randomly about and called *New Concordia Square* after the original name for the space, the monument shows in its graphic sim-plicity how the square looked after it was cleared of Jews for the last time.

GRUNWALD MONUMENT
plac Matejki; tram: 2, 4, 5, 12; map p.133 D4

Fought on 15 July 1410 by a victorious joint Polish-Lithuanian army against the Teutonic Knights, the Battle of Grunwald has gone down in history as one of the greatest battles of medieval Europe. Repre-sented in many art forms, the battle gets the full mon-ument treatment here, com-plete with a mounted King Władysław Jagiełło at the top, beneath him soldiers of both armies and, at the very bottom, a deceased Urlich von Jungingen, the Teu-

Left: meet at the Adam Mickiewicz Monument.

The **Military Cemetery** (ul. Rakowicka 26; daily 8am–dusk; free; tram: 2) is where soldiers from German, Soviet, Polish and Commonwealth armies can be found interred. The Soviet section features classic Socialist Realist memorials, as well as some of the only surviving hammer-and-sickle symbols left in the city. The well-maintained Commonwealth graveyard, one of only three in Poland, contains the graves of 483 Allied troops. The **Rakowicki Cemetery** (ul. Rakowicka 26; daily 8am–dusk; free; tram: 2) was established in 1803 and is the largest cemetery in Kraków. Here, among tree-lined pathways, eminent Poles such as artist Jan Matejko lie buried, as well as Tadeusz Pankiewicz, recognised for his selfless actions in the Kraków Ghetto (see p.16). Monuments and memorials to national uprisings are numerous, and the sepulchral art is beguiling. In Kazimierz, the **New Jewish Cemetery** (ul. Miodowa 55; Sun–Fri 9am–4pm; free; tram: 7, 9, 11, 13) dates from 1800 and is largely overgrown. This inner-city sanctuary bore the brunt of Nazi hatred, with scores of *matzevot* vandalised, opened and used for paving. A monument commemorating the Holocaust stands close to the main entrance, and fragments of broken tombs now decorate parts of the perimeter wall.

Salwator Cemetery (ul. Kościuszki 88; daily 8am–dusk; free; tram: 1) is one of Kraków's great secrets, offering grand views of the city and a peaceful atmosphere. Set on a hill, the principal point of interest to visitors is the grave of science fiction author Stanisław Lem (1921–2006).

tonic Order's Grand Master who was killed on the day. The impressive monument is a 1976 reproduction of Antoni Wiwulski's (1877–1919) 1910 original.

PŁASZÓW MEMORIAL
ul. Kamieńskiego; tram: 7, 9, 11, 13

One of several memorials on the site of the former concentration camp, this large, foreboding structure dating from 1964 features five human figures carved into a solid lump of stone. Find it at the top of the hill

Below: the stark Płaszów Memorial.

at the far northern part of the site.

TADEUSZ KOŚCIUSZKO MONUMENT
Wawel; free; tram: 3, 6, 8, 10; map p.134 B3

Designed by Leonard Marconi, and executed by sculptor Antoni Popiel, the Tadeusz Kościuszko (1746–1817) equestrian statue is one of the best-loved symbols of Kraków, with a history as colourful as the city itself. Kościuszko was considered one of Poland's greatest patriots and freedom fighters, a fact not lost on the Austrians who ruled Kraków when the statue was originally cast in 1900. Permission to erect it was repeatedly refused, and it was only when Poland gained independence a quarter of a century later that Kościuszko's likeness was finally raised. Destroyed in 1940 by the occupying Germans, the statue was finally replaced in 1960, the replica a reconciliatory gift from the city of Dresden.

Museums and Galleries

Although the vast majority of museums and galleries in and around Kraków can hardly compare to their counterparts in the West in terms of modernity or interactive features, for the sheer variety of subject matter covered there are few places in Europe to beat them. Admission prices remain ludicrously cheap (and usually payable in cash only), and are generally waived on one day of the week. Last entry is usually 30 minutes before the actual closing times noted here.

MAIN MARKET SQUARE
Historical Museum of Kraków
Rynek Główny 35; tel: 12 619 2300; www.mhk.pl; Wed–Sun 10am–5.30pm; admission charge; tram: 1, 3, 6, 8; map p.132 C2

Founded over a century ago in 1899 and housed inside a classic 17th-century burgher house, this fascinating glimpse inside the history of the city from when it received the royal charter in 1257 until the German invasion of 1939 is an absolute must-see for all visitors to the city. Among the many displays, don't miss the wonderful Fontana Room by the Italian Baldassare Fontana (1658–1729) who also designed the building, or the collection commemorating Poland's fight for independence at the end of World War I. As well as the permanent upstairs galleries, the museum also has some good temporary exhibitions on the ground floor.

Best Museums...
...for Art
Bunkier Sztuki *(see p.83)*
Czartoryski Museum *(see p.83)*
National Museum of Art *(see p.88)*
Wyspiański Museum *(see p.85)*
...for History
Celestat *(see p.86)*
Historical Museum of Kraków *(see above)*
Museum of National Remembrance *(see p.88)*
...for Science
City Engineering Museum *(see p.86)*

OLD TOWN
Archaeology Museum
ul. Poselska 3; tel: 12 422 7100; www.ma.krakow.pl; Mon–Wed 9am–2pm, Fri 10am–2pm, Sun 10am–2pm; admission charge; tram: 1, 3, 6, 8; map p.134 B4

A recommended excursion concentrating on the history and culture of the area over the last 90,000 years, among other things. Highlights include a room dedicated to the history of clothing and a handful of dark rooms full of relics from ancient Egypt. Inside

a building that's served many purposes over the centuries, including stints as a monastery and a prison, the museum's gardens, which feature a few interesting contemporary sculptures, are also worth having a look at.

Archdiocesan Museum
ul. Kanonicza 19–21; tel: 12 421 8963; www.muzeumkra. diecezja.pl; Tue–Fri 10am–4pm, Sat–Sun 10am–3pm; admission charge; tram: 3, 6, 8, 10; map p.134 C3

Aside from numerous vestments, robes and mitres, the collection in this

Left and **below left:** displays at the Historical Museum of Kraków.

Those serious about their sightseeing should invest in a **Kraków Tourist Card** (www.krakowcard.com), an excellent credit card-shaped object which not only gives the owner unrestricted access to over 30 museums and galleries but also some restaurant discounts and free rides on the city's trams and buses. Cards are valid from two to three days, are available from 50–65zł and can be bought from tourist information points and a number of hotels.

splendid building includes a 13th-century painting of St Agnes and St Catherine, Gothic sculptures of the *Virgin and Child* and a 14th-century chalice donated to the museum by the late Pope John Paul II. He resided here twice during his life, and one room has been kept just as it was before he was appointed bishop, complete with skis on the wall that once belonged to him. More Pope-related mementoes come by way of various gifts presented to him by world and Church leaders. The museum also hosts regular art exhibitions.

Bunkier Sztuki

pl. Szczepański 3a; tel: 12 422 1052; www.bunkier.art.pl; Tue–Sun 11am–6pm, Thur until 8pm; admission charge; tram: 2, 3, 4, 12; map p.132 B3
A stark, glorious and somewhat controversial communist-era reinforced concrete building that looks wonderfully out of place in the Old Town, the Art Bunker showcases tempo-

rary exhibitions of mostly conceptual art from home and abroad, including painting, sculpture and photography. One of the best places in the city for seeing contemporary art, the venue also houses an excellent café.
SEE ALSO BARS AND CAFÉS, P.32

Burgher Museum (Hippolit House)

pl. Mariacki 3; tel: 12 422 4219; www.mhk.pl; Wed–Sun 10am–17.30pm; admission charge; tram: 1, 3, 6, 8, 18; map p.133 D2

Below: the Archaeology Museum building.

Named after the illustrious 16th-century Hippolit family who once lived here, one can only imagine the bill for the furniture polish in this place. Spread out over several floors, the museum recreates a number of bourgeois residences as lived in by the top echelons of the city from the 17th to the early 20th century. Brimming with exquisite furniture and a few personal possessions, it's well worth a visit and really conjures up the spirit of the city's former elite business families.

Czartoryski Museum

ul. Św. Jana 19; tel: 12 422 5566; www.muzeum.krakow. pl; Tue–Sat 10am–6pm, Sun 10am–4pm; admission charge; tram: 2, 3, 4, 12; map p.133 C3
A truly exemplary gallery housed inside an ensemble of buildings worth seeing in their own right, this mammoth collection of outstanding art and militaria is eclipsed by Leonardo da Vinci's *Lady with an Ermine*, dating from around 1490 and one of only four

83

Left: da Vinci's famous painting *Lady with an Ermine*.

Visits are by guided tour only. Booking in advance is highly recommended.

Jan Matejko House

ul. Floriańska 41; tel: 12 422 5926; www.muzeum. krakow.pl; Tue–Sat 10am–6pm, Sun 10am–4pm; admission charge; tram: 2, 4, 7, 10; map p.133 D3

A painter of historical epics in Polish history and cherished by the nation for his nationalist outlook, Jan Matejko (1838–93) drew his first and last breath in this lavish Old Town house. Completely renovated in 2009, the museum is now better than ever, containing a treasure chest of items of interest to fans of the man and Romantic-era art in general. As well as plenty of original works including drawings and paintings by the artist himself, other items on display include personal possessions, gifts to the artist from his students and a collection of work from both East and West that made up Matejko's private collection.

Below: artworks at the Wyspiański Museum.

female portraits by the artist in existence. Drawn from the private collection of Princess Izabela Czartoryska (1746–1835), many of the exhibits come with their own fascinating stories echoing the various fates of the city.

For the uninitiated, Polish museums can be intimidating places. Here the hands-on multimedia museums of the West are largely unheard of, and instead visitors can expect to be herded around by hawk-like curators who waste no time in jumping into action should one stray too close to an exhibit. Furthermore, it's not just the displays that are considered sacred, but floors as well. Don't be surprised to be handed a pair of plastic bags or silly slippers to put round your shoes to prevent a scuffing of the hallowed parquet.

Jagiellonian University Museum

ul. Jagiellońska 15; tel: 12 422 0549; www.uj.edu.pl/muzeum; Mon–Fri 10am–3pm, Tue until 4pm, Sat 10am–2pm; admission charge; tram: 2, 3, 4, 8; map p.132 B2

Featuring a beautifully cloistered Gothic courtyard, Collegium Maius of the Jagiellonian University is the oldest educational institute in Poland, with guided tours taking visitors through a 16th-century library, the Treasury (complete with Queen Jadwiga's mace) and the Green Hall, whose attractions include a piano once played by none other than Chopin. The highlight, however, is the Copernicus Room, which includes the famous Jagiellonian Globe, dating from 1510 and believed to be the first globe produced that included the Americas.

Wyspiański Museum

ul. Szczepańska 11; tel: 12 422 7021; www.muzeum.krakow.pl; Wed–Sat 10am–6pm, Sun 10am–4pm; admission charge; tram: 2, 3, 4, 12; map p.132 B3

Stanisław Wyspiański (1869–1907) is known as Kraków's creative genius. In his relatively short life, Wyspiański not only gave the world some outstanding paintings but also found time to design beautiful stained glass and even managed to write his 1901 play, *Wesele* (The Wedding), which is considered a masterpiece of Polish drama. Inside are several rooms dedicated to the artist and his life, all of them packed with marvellous things to see, from furniture he designed for Feliks Jasieński to personal effects, and a model of his great unrealised dream for the complete renovation of Wawel.

WAWEL
Cathedral Museum

Wawel; tel: 12 429 3327; www.wawel.krakow.pl; Mon–Sat 9am–5pm; admission charge; tram: 3, 6, 8, 10; map p.134 B3

Housed inside an impressive 14th-century Gothic building next to the Cathedral, the Cathedral Museum was opened in 1978 by the then Cardinal Karol Wojtyła, who just a few weeks later became Pope John Paul II. A staggering collection of church art from around the 12th century onwards, highlights include the so-called *Kmita's Chasuble*, dating from around 1503, a 12th-century silver casket from Sicily and many other artefacts related to Polish and European Christianity.

With such a wealth of galleries and museums, sightseeing in Kraków can get expensive, so cheapskates will be heartened to learn that in Poland it's traditional for most museums to open for free once a week. Even better, a number of them choose to do this on Sunday, allowing for a maximum amount of people to file through and enrich their weekend.

Tickets allow free access to the Crypts and bell.

Crown Treasury and Armoury

Wawel; tel: 12 422 5155; www.wawel.krakow.pl; Mon 9.30am–1pm, Tue–Fri 9.30am–5pm, Sun 11am–6pm; admission charge; tram: 3, 6, 8, 10; map p.134 B3

Several rooms inside the castle complex that once stored the Polish version of the Crown Jewels have been restored to their rightful position and are now open to the public. As well as the aforementioned and highly recommended jewels on display there is also the legendary *Szczerbiec*, an original notched sword from the 12th or 13th century used during coronations, an incredible array of medieval weapons and, in the three Gothic and Renaissance cellars underneath, cannons, howitzers and reproductions of the banners captured by the victorious forces at the Battle of Grunwald in 1410.

Lost Wawel

Wawel; tel: 12 422 5155; www.wawel.krakow.pl; Mon 9.30am–1pm, Tue–Thur 9.30am–5pm, Sat–Sun 11am–6pm; admission charge; tram: 3, 6, 8, 10; map p.134 B2

Opened in 1975, Lost Wawel focuses on the presentation of artefacts dug up from numerous archaeological digs at Wawel, as well as a multimedia display recreating the building between the 10th and 12th centuries. Of the former, exhibits run the gamut from a reconstructed Renaissance kitchen to a collection of tiles that once graced the castle's stoves. The multimedia exhibit is looking a bit dated nowadays, but still does a marvellous job of helping to recreate the former splendour of this ancient site.

State Rooms and Royal Apartments

Wawel; tel: 12 422 5155; www.wawel.krakow.pl; Tue–Fri 9.30am–5pm, Sat–Sun 11am–6pm; admission charge; tram: 3, 6, 8, 10; map p.134 B3

The loss of the Polish monarchy may have been something of a blow to the Poles but it did at least open up their secret world of splendour to the general

Below: royal riches at the Crown Treasury.

public. The State Rooms feature a spectacular collection of gems and the finest examples of specially commissioned 16th-century Flemish tapestry bearing biblical scenes. Of particular interest are the magnificent Eagle Room, where the Royal Court once sat, and the Senators' Hall, the largest room in the castle, where royal weddings once took place. The Royal Apartments, which can only be visited on a guided tour, contain both bedrooms and other rooms resplendent with Renaissance furniture, as well as the oldest tapestry in the castle and breathtaking paintings.

KAZIMIERZ
City Engineering Museum
ul. Św. Wawrzyńca 15; tel: 12 421 1242; www.mimk.com.pl; Tue–Sun 10am–4pm; admission charge; tram: 7, 9, 11, 13; map p.137 D3

Housed inside a sprawling former tram depot, this exceedingly child-friendly museum, that also appeals to bigger boys who like their toys, gives over most of its space to a collection of vintage motorbikes, cars, lorries and public transport from Poland and abroad that, supposedly, aims to

chart the history of the city's automotive industry. The other permanent display worth a mention is the Fun and Science exhibit, a low-budget collection of hands-on experiments that help explain the basics behind science.

Galicia Jewish Museum
ul. Dajwór 18; tel: 12 421 6842; www.galiciajewish museum.org; daily 10am–6pm; admission charge; tram: 7, 9, 11, 13; map p.137 D4

The core of the recommended Galicia Jewish Museum consists of 140 large photographs taken by the Museum's late director, London-born Jewish photojournalist Chris Schwarz (1948–2007) during his travels across southeastern Poland. The exhibition is the result of over 12 years of work, with the photographs split into five separate themes, namely Jewish life in ruins, Jewish culture as it once was, sites of massacre and destruction, how the past is remembered and people making memory today. The trail of images is complemented by texts provided by Jonathan Webber, the Unesco Chairman of Jewish and Interfaith Studies.

Museum of Ethnography
pl. Wolnica 1; tel: 12 430 5563; www.etnomuzeum.eu; Tue–Sat 11am–7pm, Thur until 9pm, Sun 11am–3pm; admission charge; tram: 7, 9, 11, 13; map p.136 B3

Celebrating its centenary in 2011 and located inside Kazimierz's Renaissance former Town Hall, this surprisingly large and highly recommended museum on three floors was initially founded by the local folklore enthusiast Seweryn Udziela (1857–1937). Aiming to capture the spirit of local peasant arts and crafts both religious and secular, many of the marvellous exhibits of note are recreations of humble 19th-century dwellings complete with authentic folk motifs painted on the walls, items of clothing, some exceptional examples of the city's famous Nativity cribs and, on the top floor, arguably the best collection of folk art in the region, featuring some truly outstanding hand-painted wooden carvings.

AROUND THE CENTRE
Celestat
ul. Lubicz 16; tel: 12 429 3791; www.mhk.pl; Tue–Sat 9.30am–5pm; admission charge; tram: 2, 4, 5, 9

Hoodwinked somewhat amusingly by an erroneous marking on an ancient map, the szlachta, or Polish nobility, were many centuries ago led to believe they were descended from the Sarmatians, an ancient Tatar tribe from the northern Black Sea coast. Adopting the Sarmatian dress code of lavish robes

Once a year, usually in May, Polish museums throw their doors open for the evening as part of the European Night of Museums. In exchange for 1zł, members of the public can purchase a commemorative coin which in turn grants them entrance to all participating museums. With public transport laid on and doors open until around 1am, it's not unusual to find young revellers fusing drinking with culture, lending a distinctly lively angle to the sightseeing.

and handlebar moustaches, between the 16th and 19th century these horse-riding Polish bigwigs were responsible for all manner of important duties, including the defence of their cities. Enter the Fowler Brotherhood, an organisation that sprung up countrywide and practised the art of defence by shooting at chickens on the ends of long sticks. This extraordinary museum, commemorating the eccentric brotherhood which exists to this day and whose elected king worships a silver chicken, is a must-see when in town. Highlights include some remarkable portraits of former kings and the silver chicken itself.

History of Photography Museum
ul. Józefitów 16; tel: 12 634 5932; www.mhf.krakow.pl; Wed–Fri 11am–6pm, Sat–Sun 10am–3.30pm; admission charge; tram: 4, 8, 12, 13
Allegedly the only museum dedicated exclusively to photography in the country (a fact the small photogra-

phy museum in Bydgoszcz may well dispute), this rather lacklustre, old-style museum is a must for fans of photography all the same. Small even by Kraków standards, the museum is divided into two sections, including an interesting collection on the history of photography in the city courtesy of old equipment and some fine historic photographs, and a temporary exhibition space that promises anything from the outstanding to the average.

Manggha
ul. Konopnickiej 26; tel: 12 267 2703; www.manggha. krakow.pl; Tue–Sun 10am–6pm; admission charge; tram: 18, 19, 22; map p.132 A1
Over the course of his life, Japanophile Feliks Jasieński (1861–1929) amassed over 6,500 works of art from the Land of the Rising Sun, bequeathing them on his deathbed to Kraków's National Museum. However, it was only after director Andrzej Wajda donated his prize money from the 1987 Kyoto Film Festival that work began on creating a building to host the collection. Designed by the Japanese architect Arata Iszozaki, the

Above: the Manggha building.

Manggha Centre opened in 1994 and contains a wide range of Japanese treasures, from samurai armour to antique vases and silk screen paintings. Also of note is the in-house Japanese café, complete with a splendid view of Wawel over the Wisła river and a bookstore specialising in Japanese titles.

Mehoffer Museum
ul. Krupnicza 26; tel: 12 421 1143; www.muzeum.krakow.pl; Tue–Sat 10am–6pm, Sun 10am–6pm; admission charge; tram: 4, 8, 12, 13; map p.132 A3
Stanisław Wyspiański was born here in 1869, although it's another artist with whom this house will for ever be linked. Józef Mehoffer (1869–1946) was one of the leading lights of the *Młoda Polska* (Young

Right: the Celestat celebrates an eccentric tradition.

87

Right: discover Polish art at the National Museum.

Poland) movement, and from 1932 until 1946 lived here, reorganising the interiors and filling them with his paintings and stained-glass creations. The house and adjoining garden have been preserved under the guardianship of the National Museum of Kraków, and today visitors can tread through lavish chambers full of period furnishings and Mehoffer's works.

National Museum of Art

al. 3 Maja 1; tel: 12 295 5500; www.muzeum.krakow.pl; Tue–Sat 10am–6pm, Sun 10am–4pm; admission charge; tram: 15, 18

Set up in 1879 and the first museum of its kind in what was, at the time, a country that technically didn't exist, this is the main museum of a total of 10 around Kraków, and is simply one of the best in the city. Drawing on an extensive collection of almost half a million pieces, this rather grotesque-looking concrete building hides some truly outstanding work. Split into three permanent exhibitions, namely Arms and Uniforms in Poland, the Gallery of Decorative Art and 20th-Century Polish Art, spending an hour or two wandering around the three floors is time well spent indeed. The 20th-Century Polish Art exhibit on the top floor is worth a special mention and is full of work that gives credence to the city's claim to be one of the great cultural centres of Europe. Highly recommended.

Polish Aviation Museum

al. Jana Pawła II 39; tel: 12 642 8700; www.muzeumlotnictwa.pl; Mon 9am–3.30pm, Tue–Fri 9am–5pm, Sat–Sun 10am–4pm; admission charge; tram: 4, 5, 9, 10

Residing on a former airfield on the western outskirts of Nowa Huta and founded in 1964, this museum aimed squarely at enthusiasts celebrates manned flight in all its forms, from early balsawood planes to a rusting collection of Soviet-built fighter jets. Home to one of the world's few remaining Spitfires, a trip out here is worth the effort despite the sad lack of English explanations.

Silesian House

ul. Pomorska 2; tel: 12 633 1414; www.mhk.pl; Tue–Sat 10am–5.30pm; free; tram: 4, 8, 12, 13

This drab-looking building achieved prominence during World War II when it became the seat of the local Gestapo. For six years, thousands of Poles passed through here to be 'processed' and interrogated, and the basement cells contain the scribbled inscriptions of many former inmates. The second part of the museum consists of more traditional displays set on the other side of the courtyard. Covering both Nazi occupation and post-war Stalinist oppression, the museum presents visitors with a self-explanatory collection of exhibits including execution lists, uniforms and even a cigarette case made from human skin.

PODGÓRZE AND PŁASZÓW

Museum of National Remembrance

pl. Bohaterów Getta 18; tel: 12 656 5625; Tue–Sun 9.30am–5pm, Mon 10am–2pm; admission charge; tram: 7, 9, 11, 13; map p.137 E2

Better known as the Pharmacy Under the Eagles, it's from here that Gentile Tadeusz Pankiewicz (1908–93) operated under the Nazis as the sole source of medicine for Ghetto inhabitants. During this time, the pharmacy became an important centre of covert activity, and Pankiewicz has himself since been inducted into Yad Vashem's Righteous Among Nations. Spurred by donations from directors Steven Spielberg and Roman Polański, the pharmacy has been operating as a small museum since 1983 and tells the story of the Kraków Ghetto from its inception to liquidation, using displays including grainy photographs, film projections, survivor artwork and items such as Star of David armbands.

Schindler's Factory

ul. Lipowa 4; tel: 12 257 1017; Tue–Sun 10am–5.30pm; admission charge; tram: 7, 9, 11, 13

After a decade of financial woes and legal wrangling, a permanent exhibition honouring Oskar Schindler could well be unveiled in the spring of 2010, but then again, that's been said before. To be housed inside his former enamel factory, the proposed multimedia experience promises to take in Schindler's office, recreate street scenes from the Ghetto and the entrance to the Płaszów camp before finally concluding with the recorded testimonies of those who helped the Jews during the Holocaust. It sounds highly promising, but visitors should note that the creation of this museum must be one of the most protracted sagas in sightseeing history. Whether or not it will be open in 2010

remains to be seen. At the time of going to press, a small exhibition featuring Schindler's former office and little else is open to the public. Opening times are subject to change on a weekly basis.

Starmach Gallery

ul. Węgierska 5; tel: 12 656 4915; www.starmach.com.pl; Mon–Fri 11am–6pm; admission charge; tram: 3, 6, 11, 23; map p.137 D1

Purportedly the largest private gallery in Poland, the Starmach occupies a 19th-century building originally designed to serve as a place of worship for Podgórze's Jewish community. Operating as a gallery since 1997, the restored Zucker Prayer House presents changing displays of some of Poland's most influential post-war artists, including Magdalena Abakanowicz, Tadeusz Kantor and Jan Tarasin. See the website for information on upcoming shows.

NOWA HUTA
Jan Matejko Manor House

ul. Wańkowicza 25; tel: 12 644 5674; Mon–Fri 10am–2pm; admission charge; tram: 4, 16, 17, 21

Feeling flush after the sale of his painting *Batory at Pskóv*, Jan Matejko purchased this grand manor house in 1876, using it as his weekend escape from Kraków. This is where he did much of his painting, of which several originals are on show along with other personal possessions and period furniture. Formerly owned by Hugo Kołłątaj, co-author of Poland's historic constitution of 1791, this Krzesławice property was confiscated from him following his forced exile in 1763. Kołłątaj's legacy remained in the form of the magnificent park surrounding the manor, and Matejko is said to have drawn inspiration from it for many of his works. Seen as a rather unassuming two-storey, slate-roofed structure from the outside, the wooded porch is the sole existing example of Matejko's foray

A high-school dropout, Jan Matejko (1838–93) overcame early setbacks and years as a starving artist to develop into one of Poland's most admired talents, in part thanks to his staunchly nationalist outlook. Matejko is credited with some 320 oil paintings and thousands more watercolours, with most of his work following a rousing patriotic theme. Best known for pieces such as his epic 1878 *Battle of Grunwald*, Matejko mentored other Kraków greats including Józef Mehoffer and Stanisław Wyspiański. Examples of his work, most of which survived World War II thanks to the ingenuity of gallery curators, can be found in Jan Matejko Manor House. He lies buried in the Alley of the Meritorious in the city's Rakowicki Cemetery *(see Monuments, p.81).*

Below: the sombre remains of Schindler's Factory.

Currently residing in the Royal Palace at Niepołomice, some 30km (18 miles) east of the city, 2010 promises the return of the revamped Gallery of 19th-Century Polish Art on the top floor of the Cloth Hall *(see Markets, p.78)*. Among the 500-plus paintings, sketches and sculptures will be examples from some of the city's finest such as Jan Matejko, as well as one or two more obscure, albeit recommended artists.

into architecture. After years of neglect the house passed into the hands of the Friends of Fine Art in 1960, and following restoration has since reopened as a museum. The elaborate 19th-century interiors include plush wooden chests, gilded mirrors, easels, paintings and parquet floors.

Museum of the Armed Act

os. Górali 23; tel: 12 644 3517; Mon–Fri 10am–3pm; admission by donation; tram: 4, 16, 17, 21
Easily found thanks to the large tank parked outside, this dusty little gem takes its hat off to the former residents of Nowa Huta who laid down their lives for their country. With

everything labelled in Polish only and that everything being a collection of old tin hats, faded photographs and the like, it must be said that this charming little offering will quite likely be lost on most visitors, which is a shame. Definitely worth a look are the dioramas of local life under the Nazis, featuring bizarre-looking puppets in strange life-like scenes.

Nowa Huta Museum

os. Słoneczne 16; tel: 12 425 9775; www.mhk.pl; Tue–Thur 9am–5pm, Sat 10.30am–6pm; admission charge; tram: 4, 16, 17, 21
Also housing the local Tourist Information Centre, the nice people who run this place organise temporary exhibitions relating to the area, some of them really very good indeed. Worth a visit to see what's going on, the Tourist Information Centre also stocks a good selection of books about the area and publishes a free local map.

KATOWICE
Katowice
Historical Museum

ul. Szafranka 9; tel: 32 256 1810; www.mhk.katowice.pl; Tue, Thur 10am–3pm, Wed, Fri

10am–5.30pm, Sat–Sun 11am–2pm; admission charge
While the paucity of English translations will frustrate, this museum does a grand job of telling the complete story of Katowice. The seals, charters, statues and models are explanatory enough, and Katowice's rural beginnings are celebrated with more than just a smattering of agricultural tools. Industrialisation, the Silesian Uprising, war and the peace that followed, are covered in minute detail, with banners, portraits, photographs and costumes spread over a number of rooms and floors. Pride of place, however, is reserved for the dioramas presenting perfectly preserved household interiors from the 19th and 20th centuries. Compulsorily daft slippers (provided) to protect the wooden floors must be worn here.

Silesian Museum

al. Korfantego 3; tel: 32 258 5661; www.muzeumslaskie.pl; Tue–Fri 10am–5pm, Sat–Sun 11am–5pm; admission charge
Among the usual collections of archaeological finds and temporary shows, find an upstairs gallery featuring a few superb paintings, including several by Stanisław Wyspiański.

Upper Silesian Ethnographic Park

ul. Parkowa 25; tel: 32 241 0718; www.skansen.chorzow.pl; Mon 8am–4pm, Tue–Fri 9am–5pm, Sat–Sun 11am–7pm; admission charge
A highly recommended bucolic excursion at the far

Left: folk artefacts at the Tatra Mountain Museum.

western end of the mammoth Park of Culture and Recreation, this fine collection of domestic and agricultural buildings representing the main ethnographic areas of the region even comes with a fully reconstructed 18th-century wooden church. Set over 20 hectares (50 acres) of rolling grassland, quite a few of the buildings are open to the public. Summer weekends see local artisans parked up here selling their wares.

Above: traditional shoes at the Tatra Mountain Museum.

ZAKOPANE

Dr Tytus Chałubiński Tatra Mountain Museum

ul. Krupówki 10; tel: 18 201 5205; www.muzeum tatrzanskie.pl; Tue–Sat 9am–5pm, Sun 9am–3pm; admission charge

Named in honour of the Radom-born physician (1820–89) who single-handedly founded Zakopane as a resort, this classic wooden house conceals two floors of exhibits given over to the celebration of the local culture and wildlife. On the ground floor are some wonderful recreations of peasant homes as well as the usual farming implements and folk art, whilst upstairs is a small collection of stuffed animals, fossils and other examples of the region's flora and fauna.

Karol Szymanowski Museum

ul. Kasprusie 19; tel: 18 201 3493; www.atma.z-ne.pl; Tue–Sun 10am–4pm; admission charge

Considered by many the most important Polish composer of the first half of the 20th century, Karol Szymanowski (1882–1937)

lived in this classic wooden house at the end of his life between 1930 and 1936. Now a museum in his honour, there are four rooms to view, each set out with period furniture and relics from the composer's life including original scores. Displays are in Polish, but a booklet can be bought when you get your ticket.

Tatra Mountain National Park Wildlife Museum

ul. Chałubińskiego 42a; tel: 18 206 3203; Mon–Sat 8am–3pm; free

More of an information centre than a museum, there are a few exhibits in here looking at the life of the region and neighbouring mountains. The enthusiasts who run the place are an excellent source of knowledge for visitors wanting to make the most of the Tatras whether during the summer or the winter.

Władysław Hasior Gallery

ul. Jagiellońska 18b; tel: 18 206 6871; www.muzeum tatrzanskie.pl; Wed–Sat 11am–6pm, Sun 9am–3pm; admission charge

Peer into the weird world of Władysław Hasior (1928–99), local artist and eccentric, inside his former studio. The multi-level exhibition contains scores

of paintings and installations, many enhanced using mirrors, mannequins and abandoned household objects. Almost occult-like in symbolism, the pieces are dark and disturbing, and made all the more so by eerie background sounds and giant banners that flutter gently inside this spine-tingling gallery.

Zakopane Style Museum

ul. Kościeliska 18; tel: 18 201 3602; www.muzeum tatrzanskie.pl; Wed–Sat 9am–5pm, Sun 9am–3pm; admission charge

You'll hear most locals referring to this timber-cut chalet as *Willa Koliba*. Completed to a prototype design by the painter and architect Stanisław Witkiewicz (1851–1915), it became a blueprint for local architecture, and you'll see the steep-roofed style replicated across the town. Serving as a museum since 1987, the rooms contain century-old furniture and local craftwork, illustrating how life was once lived. The highlight is upstairs, where a section is devoted to the wonderfully avant-garde portraits by Witkiewicz's eccentric and tragic son, Witkacy (1885–1939), painted whilst under the influence of opium.

Music

Kraków's lack of a mega-venue means that major acts tend to swerve the city, preferring neighbouring Chorzów instead. But that's not to say Kraków is a musical desert. Home to one of the leading national opera companies, and with elegant venues aplenty, it comes as no surprise to find classical music featuring heavily on the local musical menu. The profusion of klezmer concerts reflects the local Jewish heritage, while a large student population means edgy, independent sounds thrive in Kraków's underground bars. However, jazz is the defining sound, and the local jazz bars shouldn't be missed under any circumstances.

CLASSICAL AND OPERA

Kraków's best-known ambassador of classical music is Krzysztof Penderecki (born 1933), but generally the city tends to look backwards when celebrating classical music: Chopin, Moniuszko, Paderewski, Szymankowski and Żelenski are just a few Polish heroes whose works you'll see advertised in the box offices around, with locals and tourists taking advantage of tickets that are usually priced at little more than 60zł. Note that Kraków's rich spread of churches have embraced music, with organ recitals and chamber concerts frequently held in some of the grandest.

Kraków Academy of Music

ul. Św. Tomasza 43; tel: 12 422 0455; www.amuz.krakow.pl; tram: 2, 4, 7, 10; map p.133 D2
Originally founded as a conservatory in 1888; you'll hear students, professors and alumni performing in venues that go beyond the Academy's concert hall.

Kraków Filharmonia

ul. Zwierzyniecka 1; tel: 12 429 1345; www.filharmonia.krakow.pl; box office: Mon–Fri 11am–2pm, 3–7pm, Sat–Sun one hour before performances; tram: 2, 3, 4, 8; map p.132 A1
For symphonic recitals visit the Kraków Filharmonia, housed in a neo-Baroque building, the largest concert hall in Kraków, with a repertoire that extends to children's concerts, oratorios and organ recitals.

Kraków Opera Kameralna

ul. Miodowa 15; tel: 12 430 6606; www.kok.art.pl; daily

Below: a performance at the Kraków Academy of Music.

noon–4pm; tram: 3, 6, 8, 10; map p.135 D1
In operation since 1991 and boasting a reputation as one of the most sophisticated opera ensembles in Poland. Expect plaudit-winning classics.

Opera Krakowska

ul. Lubicz 48; tel: 12 421 1630; www.opera.krakow.pl; Mon–Fri 10am–7pm, Sat–Sun two hours before performance; tram: 4, 10, 11, 14
Housed in a state-of-the-art residence completed in 2008, the opera's season runs from October to the middle of June, with summer concerts staged at venues like Wawel.

JAZZ

Kraków has a long been known for the fogged-up charms of her jazz cellar speakeasies. The post-war Stalinist order saw jazz banned outright for its Western decadence, but legalised in the wake of his death, jazz clubs flourished throughout the 1950s and 1960s, becoming a hotbed

Left: a Górale band.

Shout along to rock band covers at Lizard King.

Spodek

al. Korfantego 35; tel: 32 258 3261; www.spodek.com.pl
Katowice's Spodek has drawn big names aplenty, with everyone from Slipknot to Sting playing inside this flying saucer-shaped venue. Holding 11,500, it's certainly the most pleasing of Poland's concert halls, with excellent acoustics.

MUSIC SHOPS

High Fidelity

ul. Podbrzezie 6; tel: 0618 44 79; Mon–Fri 11am–6pm, Sat 11am–3pm; tram: 3, 6, 8, 10; map p.135 D2
Second-hand vinyl rarities, including communist-era Polish rock, as well as obscure CDs procured by a true enthusiast.

Musica Antiqua

Wawel; tel: 12 422 5155; Mon–Sat 10am–4pm; tram: 3, 6, 8, 10; map p.134 B3
A small shop selling a wide range of classical music inside the Wawel complex.

of youthful expression. The 21st century hasn't stemmed its popularity.

Harris Jazz Bar

Rynek Główny 28; tel: 12 421 5741; www.harris.krakow.pl; daily 1pm–2am; tram: 2, 4, 7, 10; map p.132 B2
Whiskered students gravitate to this maze-like cellar with a rough timber design and regular live music.

Stalowe Magnolia

ul. Św. Jana 15; tel: 12 422 8472; www.stalowemag nolie.com; Sun–Thur 6pm–2am, Fri–Sat 6pm–4am; tram: 2, 4, 7, 12; map p.133 C3
The upscale Stalowe Magnolia has the profligate air of Jazz-Age Paris, its red-lit chambers complemented with feathery flourishes.

U Muniaka

ul. Floriańska 3; tel: 12 423 1205; www.umuniaka. krakow.pl; daily 7pm–2am; tram: 2, 4, 7, 10; map p.133 C2
True connoisseurs won't be seen anywhere but U Muniaka. Established in 1992 by saxophonist Janusz

Muniak, this cellar has seen some of Poland's biggest names. Strike it lucky and you may even come across Birmingham-born violinist, and occasional Kraków resident, Nigel Kennedy, a self-professed fan.

CONTEMPORARY

The international artists who stop off in Poland tend to do so in Warsaw or the national stadium in Chorzów. Nonetheless, several bars have forged a name for excellent live gigs.

Boogie

ul. Szpitalna 9; tel: 12 429 4306; www.boogiecafe.pl; Sun–Wed 10am–2am, Thur–Sat 10am–3am; tram: 2, 4, 7, 10; map p.133 D2
A chic venue with a well-groomed crowd appreciative of the soul and fusion jazz sounds.

Lizard King

ul. Św. Tomasza 11a; tel: 0669 45 2636; www.lizardking.pl; Sun–Thur noon–3am, Fri–Sat noon–4am; tram: 2, 4, 7, 10; map p.132 C3

No trip to the Kraków region can pass without hearing the fiddles and yodels of Górale bands hailing from the Tatra mountains. Identified by their white pyjamas and black hats, these mountain folk have created a cottage industry playing in the bars and restaurants of Kraków and Zakopane. Another local form that makes its presence felt is traditional Jewish klezmer music. Nearly all the restaurants lining ul. Szeroka feature nightly performances by talented bands. Be warned, a charge (around 20zł per table) for listening will usually be added to your bill.

Nightlife

Clubbing in Kraków once meant squelching across floors whilst foundations shook to unimaginative chart noise. The city has grown up, and while the lion's share of clubs can still be found in the vaulted catacombs of Kraków's cellars, adding some disco lights and a bedroom DJ is no longer enough. Divey, lager-in-a-plastic-glass student clubs are still in abundance, but so too are cutting-edge dance floors employing dress-to-impress gate policies. An alternative club scene also thrives, and it's not difficult to discover hip happenings in trendy squat-style spaces. *See also Bars and Cafés, p.32, and Music, p.92.*

MAIN MARKET SQUARE

Budda Drink

Rynek Główny 6; tel: 12 421 6522; www.budda-drink.pl; daily noon–1am; free; tram: 2, 4, 7, 10; map p.132 C2

Noted for its Buddha Lounge sound, this courtyard gem features one of the best beer gardens in the city, and an interior seemingly inspired by the Karma Sutra. Head to the circular mezzanine to learn tricks from the pictures of couples in tantric embraces, and don't miss out on road-testing the more than hefty list of cocktails.

Mirror Club

Rynek Główny 6; tel: 0512 488 882; www.mirrorclub.pl; Thur–Sat 9pm–5am; admission charge; tram: 2, 4, 7, 10; map p.132 C2

Descend the stairs to find yourself in Mirror Club, a beautifully crafted venue with pristine white shades, mirrored surfaces and colour-changing mood lamps. Aimed at fashion casualty twentysome-

Above: enjoying a few alfresco early evening beers.

things, this place is all high vaulted ceilings and deep, ambient grooves that you might not hear unless you're flaunting your sharpest haircut.

One Club

Rynek Główny 42; tel: 12 374 1300; www.oneclub.pl; Wed 8pm–1am, Thur–Sat 8pm–4am; admission charge; tram: 2, 4, 7, 10; map p.132 C2

A more exclusive club you won't find in Kraków, so have plenty of designer name tags dangling and be ready to spend. On the ground floor it's a snow-white lounge interior, while downstairs things get clubby as untouchable ice queens wiggle to house sounds on the marble floor. This is as VIP as Kraków gets, with Swarovski crystal chandeliers casting light onto a crowd of Paris Hilton-lookalikes.

OLD TOWN

Art Café Błęde Koło

ul. Bracka 4; tel: 0722 222 069; www.blednekolo.pl; Sun–Wed 10am–1am, Thur–Sat 10am–late; free; tram: 1, 3, 6, 8; map p.132 B2

You'll hear Art Café well before you find it. Squirreled down a courtyard, here's a rare Kraków club that's up some stairs, not down, with a wall-shaking sound system that leaves your teeth rattling. Interiors are nondescript, but the spread of rooms tends to pack out at weekends once the DJ dusts off his reggae collection each Friday. Great fun on the right night.

Left: lethal flaming sambucas at Boom Bar Rush.

Boom Bar Rush

ul. Gołębia 6; tel: 12 429 3974; www.boombarrush.com; Tue–Sun 7pm–5am; admission charge; tram: 1, 3, 6, 8; map p.132 B1

A lounge-style trend den with vanilla sofas occupied by local vamps and wannabe *Big Brother* contestants. If you like your clubs to be posey, minimal and cocktail bar in ambience then turn up here to schmooze and swagger to r'n'b and disco.

Cień

ul. Św. Jana 15; tel: 12 422 2177; www.cienklub.com; Tue–Sat 9pm–6am, Sun 9pm–3am; admission charge; tram: 2, 4, 7, 10; map p.133 C3

Rated by many as the best club in town, with a lengthy line at the door to reflect this. Look your best to make it past face control, before joining Kraków's other glamorous people in a blue-lit basement which specialises in house sounds.

Folia

Rynek Główny 30; tel: 12 423 2652; www.foliaclub.pl;

Below: decadent decor at Baccarat.

It's an easy mistake to make, albeit one many people would prefer not to make. Whereas the almost universal understanding of the term 'nightclub' is a place that fittingly describes the kind of places listed on these pages, in Poland a lit-up sign saying 'Night Club' advertises a very different kind of club altogether, and we don't even mean a strip club. Although prostitution is legal in Poland, brothels aren't.

Baccarat

ul. Stolarska 13; tel: 0695 116 760; www.baccaratclub.pl; Thur–Sat 7pm–4am; admission charge; tram: 1, 3, 6, 8; map p.133 C1

If the vulgar face of affluence doesn't offend then head to Baccarat, a champagne experience and Kraków's swankiest dance den. Dripping with chandeliers and glittery trimmings, it's no surprise to find a ruthless door policy in operation which rewards the daring and the decadent. What's a little more surprising is a blanket ban on smoking, a ground-breaking initiative in a country which barely stops short of idolising the pastime.

Baroque

ul. Św. Jana 16; tel: 12 422 0106; www.baroque.com.pl; Sun–Thur 9am–midnight, Fri–Sat 9am–3am; free; tram: 2, 4, 7, 10; map p.133 C3

Kraków, generally speaking, doesn't really do cocktails, at least not well. Baroque changes that with some of the best drinks in the city, including a selection of over 100 vodkas to add local flavour to your evening. Small but perfectly formed, and decked in deep, dark colours, this luxurious-looking restaurant-cum-bar wins prizes for a cool atmosphere, as well as eye-catching lamps that cast a dim red glow over the assembled patrons. Very much a pre-club venue, with most of the assembled punters usually ending up in Cień *(see right)* down the road.

Mon–Thur 6pm–1am, Fri–Sat 5pm–3am; admission charge; tram: 2, 4, 7, 10; map p.132 B2

Putting the art into party, this curiosity is the brainwork of some local art bods, and their influence isn't hard to spot. Set down an industrial-looking metal passageway, Folia is very much a thinking man's club, with visual diversions provided by way of bizarre installations and posters. DJ sets and weird musical performances are the norm not the exception, with music encompassing less mainstream genres, such as Miami Bass and NuRave.

Frantic

ul. Szewska 5; tel: 0790 539 330; www.frantic.pl; Tue–Sat 8pm–3am; admission charge; tram: 2, 3, 4, 8; map p.132 B2

This place gets frantic all right. Featuring bare brickwork and Greek pillars, this stalwart sees every conceivable space occupied by aspiring Travoltas. Imported DJs mix the latest house sounds, and while this might not be the best club around, it is certainly one of the biggest and most popular. Stake a place in the queue early, and polish your best hip wiggles to fit in.

InBlanco

ul. Jagiellońska 6; tel: 0660 445 300; www.inblanco.com.pl; daily 2pm–5am; admission charge; tram: 2, 3, 4, 8; map p.132 B3

A classic student cellar space with leather seating and a sticky floor attributed to too many parties. Ear-numbing dance

sounds limit conversation to one-line chat-up talk, which appears just fine with the devil-may-care, no-lectures-tomorrow crowd.

Klub Pauza

ul. Floriańska 18; www.klub pauza.pl; Mon–Sat 5pm–4am, Sun 5pm–2am; admission charge; tram: 2, 4, 7, 10; map p.133 C3

A suffocating cellar space not to be confused with the upstairs bar of the same name. While the club extension of Pauza lacks the arty weirdness of its bar-style counterpart it doesn't lack any of the atmosphere, with unisex toilets often leading to surprising situations. Nights in this basement approach legendary, with blippy electro sounds played to a hypnotised crowd of zombie-like clubbers.

Łodz Kaliska

ul. Floriańska 15; tel: 12 422 7042; daily 6pm–5am; free; tram: 2, 4, 7, 10; map p.133 C2

Now for a brick cellar with a difference. Run by a Łodz-based renegade art group, ŁK's maze-like

chambers are an almost hallucinatory experience, featuring padded ceilings, chandeliers and photographs positioned at wonky angles. The overriding theme is breasts, in particular the bare breasts of Victorian-era ladies, though they do little to distract the wanton crowd of theatre-school dropouts who assemble each night to enjoy a music policy of some randomness. From the safety of an elevated platform, DJs with names such as Woody Alien and Jelly Jazz lead the party to its invariably blurry conclusion.

M Club

ul. Św. Tomasza 11a; tel: 12 431 0049; www.mclub.pl; Wed–Thur 3pm–2am, Fri–Sat 3pm–5am; free; tram: 2, 4, 7, 10; map p.132 C3

Perfect for clandestine dating, entrance to M Club is gained by ringing the door buzzer. A hostess in evening dress will beckon you in, leading you down to a basement space thoughtfully appointed with dim lights and leather banquettes.

Right: the highly-rated Cień (see p.95) is always busy.

Left: spinning popular sounds at Prozak.

Cocktails are king here, and your seduction drinks are perfectly complemented by r'n'b sounds piped in the background.

Midgard

ul. Szpitalna 38; tel: 12 429 6983; www.klubmidgard.pl; Sun–Thur 6pm–midnight, Fri–Sat 6pm–4am; admission charge; tram: 2, 4, 7, 10; map p.133 D3

While not the hot address of yesteryear, Midgard still holds its own on the club circuit, with good house sets earning it a solid reputation on the local scene. Like much of the competition, you'll find Midgard in a converted cellar and combining a modern design with plenty of exposed stone. Less snobby than the competition, that doesn't stop the natives pulling out their weekend finery and living out their supermodel dreams.

Prozak

pl. Dominikański 6; tel: 12 429 1128; www.prozak.pl; Sun–Thur 8pm–4am, Fri–Sat 8pm–6am; free; tram: 1, 3, 6, 8; map p.132 C1

Once they've finished drinking the Irish Mbassy (see Bars and Cafés, p.32) dry most foreign groups repair to Prozac, a basement club with a music policy geared towards mainstream dance sounds. For men, a strong aftershave is usually enough to secure entry, while for ladies a short skirt and lipstick smile will prove more than adequate. From there fight your way through two levels of lager-fuelled posturing and watch with interest as blinged-up lads mark their territory and compete over local blondynkas.

Rdza

ul. Bracka 3–5; tel: 0600 395 541; www.rdza.pl; Thur–Sat 7pm–4am; admission charge; tram: 1, 3, 6, 8; map p.132 B2

Long after the rest of the Old Town sleeps you'll find ul. Bracka buzzing. Pick of the venues on offer is Rdza, a well-restored dance dungeon with a reputation for attracting top DJs from both home and abroad. Expect smoothly mixed house music inside sandblasted stone walls set well below street level.

Shakers

ul. Szewska 5; tel: 12 428 5588; www.shakers.com.pl; Mon–Thur 6pm–3am, Fri–Sat 6pm–6am; admission charge; tram: 2, 3, 4, 8; map p.132 B2

If the downstairs Frantic (see opposite) owns the biggest dance floor in Kraków, then Shakers may well have the smallest. Yet what it lacks in size it makes up for in style, with an OTT interior that could have been sketched out by P Diddy. The black and gold colour combinations are popular with Kraków's new-money set, who sip theatrically fixed cocktails while disco balls glitter overhead.

Spokój

ul. Bracka 3–5; tel: 12 430 0728; www.spokoj.pl; Mon–Thur 10am–2am, Fri 10am–4am, Sun noon–4am, Sun noon–2am; free; tram: 1, 3, 6, 8; map p.132 B2

The word is retro here, with zany primary colours and the sort of seats

Clubbing in Kraków has become an increasingly elitist sport, and those wishing to mix with the bold and beautiful are expected to be bold and beautiful themselves. Doors to the premier dance floors are vigilantly guarded by door selectors who take fiendish delight in culling the wheat from the chaff, and a foreign accent is no longer enough to secure entry. Sharp haircuts and clothes that scream money are advised, as is a reasonably sober nature. If you're staying in a five-star, circumvent problems by getting the concierge to put you on the guest list.

you'd have once seen Warhol and Hockney perched on. Music slots in with the surroundings, with funky soul and disco sounds evoking a sense of 1970s excess. The emphasis is on fun here, with none of the untouchable club queens who clip-clop around Kraków's more high-profile venues.

KAZIMIERZ
Funky Music Bar
ul. Estery 14; tel: 12 421 3470; daily 6pm–2am; free; tram: 7, 9, 11, 13; map p.135 E1
Nights can get heated in Funky, a subterranean den whose entrance is marked by an illuminated piano hanging over the staircase. It's about music not fashion here, with DJs spinning funk and soul grooves to a loud crowd clattering into walls lined with velvet trim and snapped vinyl records.

Kawiarnia Naukowa
ul. Jakuba 29–31; tel: 0602 103 526; daily 6pm–3am; free; tram: 7, 9, 11, 13; map p.135 E1
Wonderfully out-of-sync with the new look Kazimierz, the black depths of Kawiarnia Naukowa can surely be considered the home of Kraków sub-culture. As the peeling posters attest, if it's weird, it'll get played, and it shouldn't come as a surprise to find some of the most abstract bands and DJs in Kraków plying their leftfield sounds in this scruffy-looking venue.

Lokator
ul. Krakowska 27; www. lokator.pointblue.com.pl; daily 10am–1am; free; tram: 3, 6, 8, 10; map p.136 B3
A cult venue whose clien-

tele appears to dress in black and black alone. Aimed at the hard-smoking non-conformist, Lokator is something of an impromptu cultural centre promoting art exhibitions, alternative film and independent media among other highbrow causes. Arty black-and-white photographs cling to scarlet walls, while other design touches include a piano propped against a wall. The sounds match the setting, with dark moody offerings from intense-looking DJs and musicians.

Taawa
ul. Estery 18; tel: 12 421 0600; www.taawa.pl; Tue–Thur 7pm–4am, Fri–Sat 9pm–6am; admission charge; tram: 7, 9, 11, 13; map p.135 E1
Marking the area's merger with the mainstream is the opening of Taawa, a glitzy club with zappy laser lights and flock-style wallpaper patterns etched onto glass. Here it's all back-lit bars and plush furnishings, and a strict entry policy ensures most Kazimierz slackers will never get past the velvet rope.

AROUND THE CENTRE
Kijów Klub
al. Krasińskiego 34; tel: 12 422 3677; www.kijowklub.pl; Thur 4pm–2am, Fri–Sat 4pm–3am; admission charge; tram: 15,18
The owner's penchant for green is impressive, frightening almost, with Kermit colours dominating the decor in this snappy-looking club. Left of centre it might be, but a line-up of Kraków's best house DJs means quiet nights are rarely an option, and it's yet another place where you'll need a nice pair of shoes to make it through the door.

Left: lively, subterranean action at Rdza *(see p. 97).*

Kitsch

ul. Wielopole 15 (2nd floor); 7pm–late; free; tram: 1, 7, 10, 13; map p.135 E4

The party starts late and ends even later in Kitsch, a club with a reputation for the most reckless nights in town. The dance floor packs out like a tin of sardines, with classic *Boogie Nights* disco played to a sweaty audience of anything-goes clubbers. Feeling brave? The toilets are a unique if not particularly pleasurable sensory experience.

Łubu Dubu

ul. Wielopole 15 (1st floor); tel: 0694 461 402; 8pm–late; free; tram: 1, 7, 10, 13; map p.135 E4

Walls shake and drip with condensation in Łubu Dubu, a Bacchanalian destination with mangy furnishings and retro fittings. Found on the first floor of the legendary Wielopole 15, the music here is every bit as mixed as the design. Depending on his mood you'll find the DJ commit-ting to anything from sing-along disco to hits of the 1980s, and the crowd are acknowledged as the most approachable in town. It's likely you will wake up owning squiggly new numbers written in haste on scraps of paper.

KATOWICE
Elektro

pl. Sejmu Śląskiego 2; tel: 32 785 7054; www.jazzclub.pl; Sun–Thur 4pm–midnight, Fri–Sat 4pm–2am; admission charge

As the name implies, Elektro caters to the type of clubber who likes their music non-acoustic and who prefers to stay sitting down when listening to it. Large, dark and moody, and with a distinctly industrial look to the place, it's well worth checking out, and if it's not happening here you can always check out their jazz venue, Jazz Club Hipnoza, next door.

Cogiatur

ul. Gliwicka 9a; tel: 0515 267 696; www.cogitatur.pl; Tue–Thur 3pm–4am, Fri–Sat

The final word in hedonism goes to the grotty-looking building on ul. Wielopole 15. Occupied by four clubs, including the legends that are Kitsch and Łubu Dubu *(see left)*, this three-floored party den is a Kraków rite of passage, as well as a safe bet if you're searching for that elusive 6am beer. The clubs look shabby as the tenement they're in, but seldom disappoint in the debauchery stakes. Better still, with no clothes police or admission charges, Kraków's biggest party is accessible to all. Just don't make plans for the morning.

3pm–4am; admission charge

Above as well as part of an edgy café-bar of the same name, nights inside this sweaty concrete den of delinquency range from live music to an eclectic choice of DJs. Not always exactly buzzing; check the website for information on events.

ZAKOPANE
Ampstrong

ul. Jagiellońska 18; tel: 18 201 2904; www.ampstrong.org.pl; daily 7pm–4am; admission charge

Requiring something of an epic safari to find the place, hidden in a park underneath a large grey building is Amp-strong, a collection of small dark rooms decorated with spray paint and, more often than not, throbbing with cutting-edge people and a good mix of DJs. Ampstrong also doubles as a gallery and underground cinema. An excellent choice when in town.

Left: dancing at the alternative and arty Lokator.

Parks and Gardens

Kraków provides ample opportunity for spending time outdoors, with a total of 42 parks, including the Old Town-encircling Planty. Perfect for everything from picnics to bird-spotting to rollerblading, the city's green spaces are an excellent way of escaping the madness of the annual summer tourist deluge. Add to this concoction some genuine wilderness in the shape of the nearby Tatra National Park, a haven for wildlife long lost to Western Europe, and it's easy to see why Kraków is so popular.

OLD TOWN
Planty
Encircling the Old Town; tram: 1, 2, 3, 4; map p.132–5
Covering an area of about 21 hectares (52 acres) and comprising some 30 individual gardens, the lovely Planty park that stretches a total of 6km (4 miles) around the entire edge of the Old Town was formed in the space that once occupied the area between the city's two defensive walls after they were knocked down by the occupying Austrians in the first half of the 19th century. Overflowing with flowers, statues and lively outdoor cafés during the summer, the Planty provides a readily accessible escape from the tourist hordes and is an excellent spot for a walk or a picnic.

AROUND THE CENTRE
Błonia
al. Marszałka F Focha; tram: 15, 18
Not far west of the city centre and next to the National Museum of Art

(see Museums and Galleries, p.88), the 48-hectare (118-acre) Błonia began life in the 12th century as land belonging to local monks. Until relatively recently the park was mostly swampland and wasn't fully drained until sometime during the 19th century. Basically a vast meadow with little in the way of facilities, the park has a history of hosting large events from the showy displays of Napoleonic troops to the more recent Masses held by the late Pope John Paul II between 1979 and 2002. Nowadays the park stages outdoor concerts

and is a popular place for joggers and picnic-lovers.

Botanical Gardens
ul. Kopernika 27; tel: 12 663 3619; www.ogrod.uj.edu.pl; daily 9am–7pm; admission charge; tram: 9, 10, 13, 14
About 10 hectares (25 acres) in size and the oldest botanical gardens in the country, the city's highly recommended Botanical Gardens have been charming visitors since 1783. Divided into themed areas and with a small pond in the middle, the gardens also contain three hothouses where all manner of exotic species can be

Left: the Planty in winter.

From April through to September the city's Botanical Gardens play host to regular evening classical concerts, featuring everything from choirs to full chamber orchestras. The gardens also put on the occasional art exhibition and are regular supporters of the annual Museum Night. For more information about what's on, see their excellent website at www.ogrod.uj.edu.pl.

viewed. Known for being the launch site of the first hot-air balloon ever to take to the skies in Poland, just a year after the gardens were opened, the park is also home to a gnarled, 500-year-old oak tree. There's also a small museum located inside the grand manor house next to the entrance.

H Jordana Park
al. 3 Maja; tram: 15, 18
Immediately north of the Błonia and about half the size, this is the place to take the kids if they need to let off steam. A classic city park, H Jordana features an adventure playground, cycle lanes and a small lake in the middle where rowing boats can he hired.
SEE ALSO CHILDREN, P.41

Kraków Zoo and Zoological Gardens
ul. Kasy Oszczędności Miasta Krakowa 14; tel: 12 425 3551; www.zoo-krakow.pl; daily

Left: in the lovely Botanical Gardens.

9am–6pm; admission charge; bus: 134
Officially 278 species live here, among them Indian elephants, sea lions and plenty of badly behaved primates. Surprisingly well kept for an Eastern European zoo, the place has been in business since 1929 and is set in the lovely semi-wild area known as Las Wolski, which includes everything from picnic parks to small forests perfect for hiking about in. A 30-minute trip from the centre, bus 134 leaves from the first stop on the right going west along al. Marszałka F. Focha, not far from the entrance to the National Museum of Art.
SEE ALSO CHILDREN, P.41

PODGÓRZE AND PŁASZÓW
Bednarski Park
Far southern end of ul. Legionów Piłsudskiego; tram: 18, 19, 22
Laid out at the end of the 19th century when Podgórze was still a separate town, the 7.2-hectare

(18-acre) Bednarski Park was officially opened to the public on 19 July, 1896. Set amidst rolling hills, the park is a rough affair, with plants growing wild, small limestone cliffs, over 100 different species of trees and the remains of an Austrian fort, there's nothing of the manicured formality of the classic city park here. A few paths have been laid out, making the park a suitable place for cyclists.

KATOWICE
Tadeusz Kościuszko Park
ul. Kościuszki
At 72 hectares (178 acres), this large expanse of green is the biggest park in Katowice proper. Featuring over 90 varieties of trees, plants and shrubs including azaleas, beech, cherry, linden and rhododendrons and even an English rose garden, the park is popular with all manner of locals. Surplus to the flora are the recommended Church of St Michael the Archangel, an intriguing parachute tower used by Polish soldiers between the wars, a sculpture garden and a well-preserved Soviet soldiers' cemetery.

Restaurants

At first glance, Kraków reveals a wide range of restaurants and world cuisines. However, a general aversion to spices, a lack of top-quality ingredients and a sometime shortage of skilled staff make dining in Kraków a gamble, and this is especially true when choosing ethnic options. The good news is that inroads have been made, most impressively in the Italian and sushi sectors, and whilst most eateries have yet to conquer more unusual cuisines, they've certainly mastered their own. Extravagant meals of grilled meats and game abound, and with prior research fine dining is never too far away. *See also Food and Drink, p.60.*

MAIN MARKET SQUARE
Pod Krzyżkiem
Rynek Główny 39; tel: 12 433 7010; www.podkrzyzykiem. com; Mon–Thur 10am–11pm, Fri–Sun 10am–midnight; €€€; tram: 2, 4, 7, 12; map p.132 C2
Kraków dining gets the surrealist treatment in Pod Krzyżkiem, a square-located eatery with a glass floor placed over a model of the Old Town and stained glass arrangements mimicking those in neighbouring St Mary's. On the menu are modern interpretations of classic Polish cuisine which consistently elicit praise from local foodies in the know.

Redolfi
Rynek Główny 38; tel: 12 423 0579; www.redolfi.krakow.pl; daily 9am–11pm; €€€; tram: 2, 4, 7, 12; map p.132 C2

Prices for an average three-course meal with wine:	
€€€€	over 200zł
€€€	100–200zł
€€	50–100zł
€	under 50zł

Above: the highly rated Pod Krzyżkiem.

Calling itself French but really much more besides, Redfolfi dishes up superlative food from breakfast (of which there are three types to choose from) until bedtime. Redolent of a small-town French bistro, the interior is refreshingly scruffy, belying dishes that are anything but. Try the roast duck with mushrooms.

Szara
Rynek Główny 6; tel: 12 421 6669; www.szara.pl; daily 11am–11pm; €€€; tram: 2, 4, 7, 12; map p.132 C2

Long feted as one of the top restaurants in town, Szara impresses with its vaulted ceilings and impeccable interiors as well as a menu involving such luxuries as *foie gras* fried in honey. Black-tie service caters to a largely foreign clientele inside a venue which seldom fails to draw a full house.

Wentzl
Rynek Główny 19; tel: 12 429 5712; www.wentzl.pl; daily 1–11.30pm; €€€€; tram: 1, 3, 6, 8; map p.132 C2
Inside a 15th-century burgher house, this wonder comes with antique wooden ceilings and an impressive international menu featuring such imaginative-sounding fare as turbot with ratatouille. Certainly not for backpackers or stags, this is a place to push the culinary boat out in style.

Wesele
Rynek Główny 10; tel: 12 422 7460; www.wesele restauracja.pl; daily 10am–

Left: Wierzynek is one of Kraków's top restaurants.

Restaurants, like so many other businesses in Poland, employ a largely laissez-faire approach to their opening times. Hours listed on the door are flexible, and most premises will close early or remain open late depending on the foot flow crossing the threshold. To confuse things further, while some bolt their doors on national holidays, other restaurants (usually the most unlikely candidates) remain steadfastly open. In short, if you wish to avoid disappointment, call ahead.

11pm; €€€; tram: 1, 3, 6, 8; map p.132 C2

Even in a square lauded for its restaurants, Wesele stands out as something special. Rustic interiors feature plenty of flowers and carpentry, while the food scores highly for fantastic translations of local dishes. The goose is a highlight, although those wishing to sample it might want to book a table ahead.

Wierzynek

Rynek Główny 15; tel: 12 424 9600; www.wierzynek.pl; daily 1–11pm; €€€€; tram: 1, 3, 6, 8; map p.132 C1

Kraków's most famous restaurant, with a history that goes back to 1364 and a guestbook that includes Robert de Niro, Kate Moss and Fidel Castro. Divided into formal-looking dining rooms, this Kraków must is a bank-breaker by local standards, though the resultant guinea fowl, venison and boar are very much worth the considerable expense.

OLD TOWN
Amarone

ul. Floriańska 14; tel: 12 424 3381; www.hotel.com.pl; daily noon–11pm; €€€€; tram: 2, 4, 7, 10; map p.133 C3

Set under a glass atrium, the Michelin-recommended Amarone features divine Italian creations courtesy of head chef Alfredo Chiocchetti, as well as homemade pasta and bread baked on the premises. Furnished in a chic fashion, with chequered flooring and swooning palms, it's defi-

Below: service with a smile at Wentzl.

nitely a favourite for romantic repasts and expense-claim dinners.

Balaton

ul. Grodzka 37; tel: 12 422 0469; www.balaton.krakow.pl; daily noon–10pm; €€; tram: 3, 6, 8, 10; map p.134 C4

Stuffed peppers and fiery goulashes are the mainstay of this veteran restaurant, and deserve particular praise in a city that prefers to pander to the timid Polish palate. In a certain light Balaton can appear tired and shabby, but that changes when the sun sets and Roma bands stroll between candlelit tables.

Bar Grodzki

ul. Grodzka 47; tel: 12 422 6807; www.grodzkibar.zaprasza.net; Mon–Sat 9am–7pm, Sun 10am–7pm; €€; tram: 3, 6, 8, 10; map p.134 C4

Hearty Polish fare with plenty of shredded cabbage in a choice of halls, from the not exactly salubrious ground-floor canteen-looking space to the more upscale vaulted brick cellar below. The good-value food comes in gut-busting proportions guaranteed to keep visitors full for hours.

Carlito
ul. Floriańska 28; tel: 12 429 1912; www.restauracjacarlito.pl; daily 10am–11.30pm; €€; tram: 2, 4, 7, 10; map p.133 D3
Pizza is the forte in Carlito, a vast space which hums with custom early or late. With its ochre walls and trattoria style, it's a welcome departure from the standard Old Poland offerings, and the open kitchen is a frequent source of amateur dramatics. During the summer season check the rooftop terrace to view the human flotsam that floods down ul. Floriańska.

Chimera Salad Bar
ul. Św. Anny 3; tel: 12 292 1212; www.chimera.com.pl; daily 10am–11pm; €€; tram: 1, 3, 6, 8; map p.132 B2
Aristocratic 19th-century Polish dishes in four atmospheric halls; surplus to the plethora of grilled meat and vegetarian

Above: Carlito is a top choice for pizza.

dishes is the legendary mammoth salad bar, a popular favourite among locals and tourists alike. The summer terrace gets packed during the day and is a great place to fill up and watch the world drift by.

Cyrano de Bergerac
ul. Sławkowska 26; tel: 12 411 7288; www.cyranodeberg erac.pl; Mon–Sat 10am–11pm €€€€; tram: 2, 4, 7, 10; map p.132 C4
Discerning diners flock to Cyrano, a high-class establishment which rewards big spenders with some of the best meals in Poland. Set in an arched brick cellar, the lavish design is complemented by superb Chateaubriand and simpering service. Book a table well in advance and make sure you've got plenty of money in the bank before you order.

Green Way
ul. Mikołajska 14; tel: 12 431 1027; www.greenway.pl; Mon–Fri 10am–10pm, Sat–Sun 11am–9pm; €€; tram: 2, 4, 7, 10; map p.133 D2
Poland's number one vegetarian restaurant sees bespectacled students and old ladies jostle at the

counter over some of the best non-meat-based dishes in town. Some of the food on offer is a bit hit and miss, but for affordable fare that never hurt a fly, Green Way is a tough one to beat.

Indus Tandoor
ul. Sławkowska 13–15; tel: 12 423 2282; www.indus.pl; Sun–Thur noon–10pm, Fri–Sat noon–midnight; €€; tram: 2, 4, 7, 10; map p.132 C3
Yet to be granted truly great Indian food, those hankering for curry in Kraków make do in Indus, a long, narrow eatery with imported chefs and images of Ganesh on the walls. Calmed-down recipes reflect years of catering to local taste, so make sure to impress the sari-clad servers if you need an extra kick to your order.

Kalinka
ul. Gertrudy 7; tel: 12 422 3257; www.kuchniarosyjska.com; daily noon–10pm; €€€; tram: 3,

Even in Kraków, a city swamped with tourists, service can remain surprisingly Cold War-esque. Whilst English-speaking staff are now the norm, efficient service isn't. Tipping, if warranted, should either be the international 10 percent, or the zero of your choosing. Diners should also be aware when paying. A word of thanks when a waiter retrieves the bill is sometimes interpreted as a sign to keep the change. Avoid embarrassing situations by saving your gratitude once change has arrived before tipping accordingly.

Prices for an average three-course meal with wine:
€€€€	over 200zł
€€€	100–200zł
€€	50–100zł
€	under 50zł

6, 8, 10; map p.135 D4
With its faded air and
Orthodox icons, Kalinka is
all deep-red sofas and old
Russian ambience. The
blini with caviar are
particularly noteworthy,
with new courses best
greeted with ice-cold
vodka as balalaikas stir in
the background.

La Campana
ul. Kanonicza 7; tel: 12 430
2232; www.lacampana.pl; daily
noon–11pm; €€€; tram: 3, 6, 8,
10, 18; map p.134 C4
Any visit here is likely to be
repeated. With its light timber touches and Laura
Ashley patterns, La Cam-
pana gets 10 out of 10 for
design before going posi-
tively off the scale for its
food. Start with baked
pear cooked with cran-
berry mousse, before mov-
ing on through a menu
touting linguine and lamb.

La Fontaine
ul. Sławkowska 1; tel: 12 422
6564; www.bblafontaine.com;
daily noon–11pm; €€€; tram: 2,
4, 7, 10; map p.132 C3
Francophiles convene at
La Fontaine, a labyrinthine
venue occupying a 13th-
century cellar. Adding
class to Kraków's culinary
chart is the up-and-
coming French chef, with
morel mushrooms and *foie
gras* part of his perfectly
formed repertoire.

Leonardo
ul. Szpitalna 20–22; tel: 12 429
6850; www.leonardo.com.pl;
daily 11am–11pm; €€€; tram:
2, 4, 7, 10; map p.133 D3
Dine in the Leonardo
Salon, adorned with da
Vinci's scientific designs,

or in the Wine Chamber,
with rough-hewn walls
and country kitchen-style
trappings. The chef here
is prone to invention, and
his signature dish, veni-
son wrapped in Italian
bacon, warrants thorough
investigation.

Metropolitan
ul. Sławkowska 3; tel: 12 421
9803; www.metropolitan-
krakow.com; Mon–Sat
7.30am–midnight, Sun
7.30am–10pm; €€€; tram: 2, 4,
7, 10; map p.132 C3
Famed for its artery-clogging English breakfast,
which is certainly the best
thing they get up to in the
open kitchen, Metropolitan
boasts a great location just
off the square, friendly if
sometimes forgetful wait-
resses and the occasional
group of chess players. A
classic Old Town favourite.

Miód i Wino
ul. Sławkowska 32; tel: 12 422
7495; www.hawelka.pl; daily
11am–11pm; €€€; tram: 2, 4, 7,
10; map p.133 C4
A good choice to fill hun-
gry faces amidst suits of
armour and stuffed animal
heads, this medieval-feel
favourite comes complete
with waiting staff in traditional costumes and an

Above: the chessboard awaits
at Metropolitan.

extensive menu to leave all
but the most ravenous
feeling satisfied. Try the
classic *żurek* soup, a
national classic made from
fermented rye flour.

Miód Malina
ul. Grodzka 40; tel: 12 430
0411; www.miodmalina.pl;
daily noon–11pm; €€€; tram: 3,
6, 8, 10; map p.134 C4
Bookings are advised in
Miód Malina, a romance-
never-dies venue with a
log fire and rural decor.
Here's tourist Kraków at its
best. You won't hear local
accents on the table next
door, and you can't expect
service always to be atten-
tive, but the Polish-Italian
menu never disappoints
with its plum sauce duck
and Polish meat platters.

Right: travel back to medieval
Poland at Miód i Wino.

Sakana

ul. Św. Jana 8; tel: 12 429
3086; www.sakana.pl; daily
noon–11pm; €€€; tram: 2, 4, 7,
12; map p.133 C3
The perfect antidote if all
those *pierogi* have swelled
the beltline. Wooden boats
carrying sushi swim past
diners in this standout
Japanese offering as
upwardly mobile Poles
practise deft chopstick
moves amid *shoji* screens
and Japanese ceramics.

Stary Hotel Restaurant

ul. Szczepańska 5; tel: 12 384
0806; www.stary.hotel.com.pl;
daily noon–11pm; €€€€; tram:
2, 4, 7, 10, 40; map p.132 B3
Gorgeous surroundings,
exquisitely presented Polish food with a distinct
international twist, a small
selection of fine European
wines and a bill at the end
of it all to leave you doing
the washing up for weeks.
Unlike most hotel restau-
rants, the Stary gets everything just right from soup
through to nuts.

U Babci Maliny

ul. Sławkowska 17; tel: 12 422
7601; www.kuchniaubabci
maliny.pl; €€; tram: 2, 4, 7, 10;
map p.132 C3
Fiendishly tucked away in

> Born in the communist era,
> Poland's contribution to the
> fast-food industry is the
> *zapiakanka*, a halved baguette
> topped with cheese, mush-
> rooms and ketchup, before
> benefiting from a stint in the
> microwave. Kraków is particu-
> larly famous for this culinary
> creation, with the hatchways
> inside plac Nowy's rotunda
> building earning a name for the
> best (and most experimental)
> ones in the city.

a courtyard and down a
flight of stairs, this is fairy-
tale Polish dining at its
most extreme. Despite
pandering to the tourists,
the food is well above par
and the prices surprisingly
reasonable. Go for a plate
of steaming *pierogi* before
clambering onto the bed in
the corner to sleep it all off.

Zapiecek Polski Pierogarnie

ul. Sławkowska 32; tel: 12 422
7495; www.zapiecek.eu; daily
24 hours; €; tram: 2, 4, 7, 10;
map p.133 C4
Recently falling into the
hands of a national chain
but still upholding its ter-
rific standards, this ridiculously small affair keeps all
manner of diners happy

with plastic plates of
pierogi handmade on the
premises. A good place to
make new friends, having
a table to yourself is
unthinkable here.

Zen

ul. Św. Tomasza 29; tel: 12 426
5555; www.zensushi.pl; daily
noon–11pm; €€€; tram: 2, 4, 7,
10; map p.133 D2
On the ground floor, visitors snap up sushi sets as
they float by on boats,
while upstairs it's shoes off
and legs crossed as diners
sit in proper Japanese
style on mats and cush-
ions. The raw fish is highly
rated, but for the real gour-
met experience prepare to
spend big for the hand-
massaged Kobe beef.

KAZIMIERZ
Al Dente

ul. Kupa 12; tel: 12 430 0418;
www.aldente-krakow.com;
daily noon–11pm; €€€; tram: 7,
9, 11, 13; map p.135 E1
Al Dente's chief claim to
fame is the largest choice
of pasta in Kraków, and
you'll find many locals professing this to be their
favourite Italian in town.
Sardinian chef Mario has
created a masterpiece
here, with urbane, ice-
white interiors completing
a memorable experience.

Bagelmama

ul. Dajwór 10; tel: 12 346 1646;
www.bagelmama.com;
Mon–Sat 9am–9pm, Sun
9am–7pm; €; tram: 7, 9, 11, 13;
map p.137 D4
Budget eating doesn't get
any better. Run by a
Chicago exile who cooks
for John McEnroe when-
ever he's covering the

Left: preparing a table at the
Stary Hotel Restaurant.

Left: fresh, seed-topped bagels at Bagelmama.

ting topped off with Jewish delicacies like czulent and goose necks.

Paroles Paroles

pl. Wolnica 4; tel: 12 423 2424; www.paroles.pl; daily 11am–10pm; €€€; tram: 3, 6, 8, 10; map p.136 C3

There's a cold, stark aesthetic in this place, accentuated further by granite flooring and a wall of smashed stones. It's certainly modern if not welcoming, while the menu is absolutely experimental by Kraków standards. Try dishes like tuna steak served with onion chutney, or duck drumsticks in balsam sauce.

Pepe Rosso

ul. Kupa 15; tel: 12 431 0875; www.peperosso.pl; daily noon–11pm; €€€; tram: 7, 9, 11, 13; map p.135 E1

A good all-round Kazimierz choice, Pepe Rosso tempts the taste buds with a wide range of handsome Italian dishes to be digested on one of two floors, depending on your smoking preference. The reasonably priced pasta and risotto dishes are particularly good here, although there's plenty more on the menu if you want it.

Polakowski

ul. Miodowa 39; tel: 12 421 0776; www.polakowski.com.pl; daily 9am–10pm; €; tram: 3, 6,

French Open, this place serves sweet and savoury bagels as well as a smattering of Tex Mex dishes. The chicken burritos, served as hot as you wish, come highly endorsed by Kraków's ever-expanding American community.

Dawna Temo Na Kazimierzu

ul. Szeroka 1; tel: 12 421 2117; daily 10am–11pm; €€€; tram: 7, 9, 11, 13; map p.135 E2

Disguised to appear like a row of 19th-century hardware stores, this restaurant comes splashed with thrift-store curiosities and a menu directly inspired by local Jewish traditions. It's best to come at night, when candlelight illuminates an antique interior filled with sewing machines and mannequins.

Deli Bar

ul. Meiselsa 5; tel: 12 430 6404; www.delibar.pl; Mon–Thur 11am–10pm, Fri–Sun 11am–11pm; €€; tram: 3, 6, 8, 10; map p.136 B4

A pleasant minimalist feel with the added bonus of a good summer terrace, Hungarian food never tasted this good, at least not in Poland. In addition

to a knockout spicy goulash, among the other excellent-value dishes here are some great salads, soups and even a decent selection of wine.

Edo

ul. Bożego Ciała 3; tel: 12 422 2424; www.edosushi.pl; Sun–Wed noon–10pm, Thur–Sat noon–11pm; €€€; tram: 3, 6, 8, 10; map p.135 D1

Kraków's original sushi stop, and quite possibly its best. Featuring a Zen-like calm, trips to Edo should begin with a cleansing miso soup before ordering expertly prepared sashimi in the rice-paper-panelled back room.

Klezmer Hois

ul. Szeroka 6; tel: 12 411 1245; www.klezmer.pl; daily 9am–9.30pm; €€€; tram: 7, 9, 11, 13; map p.135 E2

The address, at the top of ul. Szeroka, appears to confirm its tourist-trap credentials, but it is certainly worth a visit, even more so when musicians launch forth into lively klezmer recitals. Filled with gramophones and oil paintings, everything in here creaks and wobbles, with the charismatic set-

Prices for an average three-course meal with wine:	
€€€€	over 200zł
€€€	100–200zł
€€	50–100zł
€	under 50zł

107

8, 10; map p.135 E2
Grab a tray, join the queue, then scoop out meat and veg from steaming-hot containers before settling down with low-cost diners eating the local way. Operating since 1899, the *bigos* here is as legendary as the venue. Distinguishing Polakowski from the classic milk bar experience are an English menu, countryside decorations and a toilet that flushes.

Formerly run as state-sponsored canteens, the phenomenon that is the milk bar *(bar mleczny)* has yet to die. Seen as relics of the communist era, eating in one couldn't be simpler. Join a queue, point at what you want, then retreat to a plastic table after a gruff lady has plopped whatever you've apparently ordered onto a plate. Very cheap, and occasionally cheerful, expect lots of cabbage-like smells, mysterious hatchways, little English and a Dickensian selection of characters. Truly an unique side of Poland most visitors foolishly forgo.

AROUND THE CENTRE
Bar Smak
ul. Karmelicka 10; tel: 12 431 2149; daily 11am–10pm; €; tram: 4, 8, 12, 13; map p.132 A3
This quintessentially Polish venue is brimming with local flavour, some of it in the food but most of it in the characters who eat here. An English menu is thankfully available, and the wide choice of Polish food is both ridiculously cheap and highly recommended.

Burrito Buffet
ul. Warszawska 20; tel: 12 633 0409; www.burritobuffet.com.pl; Mon–Fri 10am–9pm, Sat–Sun 11am–9pm; €; tram; 12,19
The desperate standard of Kraków's ethnic options allows the entry of Burrito Buffet, a cut-price takeaway where plates (and tables) are at a premium. Marked by illuminated sombreros hanging outside, the resulting burritos are a revelation, with superhuman portions doused in dynamite sauce consumed on the swivelly stools by the wall.

Chłopskie Jadło
ul. Św. Agnieszki 1; tel: 12 421 8520; www.chlopskiejadlo.pl; Sun–Thur noon–10pm, Fri–Sat noon–11pm; €€; tram: 3, 6, 8, 10; map p.135 C1
Ocean-blue walls hung with hams and pitchforks announce Chłopskie Jadło, a nationwide enterprise which has the tourist market cornered. Watch how the hefty wooden tables sink as plates of skewered animals are lowered onto them by girls dressed as country maids.

Jarema
pl. Matejki 5; tel: 12 429 3669; www.jarema.pl; daily noon–midnight; €€€; tram: 2, 4, 5, 12; map p.133 D4
Classic Polish dishes mostly hailing from the so-called 'Lost Territories' that are now parts of Ukraine, Belarus and Lithuania. Feast on beetroot soup *(barszcz)* and Lithuanian lamb overlooking the impressive Grunwald Monument *(see also Monuments, p.80)*, while listening to the occasional sound of live folk music.

Left: try out some classic folk dishes at Ogniem i Mieczem.

Momo
ul. Dietla 49; tel: 0609 685 775; daily 11am–8pm; €; tram: 18, 19, 22; map p.135 D1

The only vegan restaurant within a day's drive of the city, Momo's formula of brown rice, Indian-themed fare and other hippie-associated dishes may be familiar to many but for this part of the world it's almost unheard of. A simple canteen affair, the food is pretty good and great value considering they have the monopoly on what they're doing.

Ogniem i Mieczem
pl. Serkowskiego 7; tel: 12 656 2328; www.ogniemi mieczem.pl; Mon–Sat noon– 11pm, Sun noon–9.30pm; €€; tram: 3, 6, 11, 23

At first glance a bit of a theme park, this amazing wooden creation is in actual fact a serious business with food based on classic old local dishes. Start the adventure with a platter of traditional lard and hunks of fresh bread then delve into a menu stuffed with large animal-based meals served on hefty wooden plates.

Pod Baranem
ul. Gertrudy 21; tel: 12 429 4022; www.podbaranem.com; daily noon–10pm; €€€; tram: 3, 6, 8, 10; map p.135 C3

A classic local experience, with meals beginning with generous helpings of lard-smeared bread. There's very much a focus on the hunter-gatherer guest, with a meat-heavy menu

Right: Pod Baranem is a serious meat-lovers' heaven.

presented inside a stone-clad space adorned with faded flowers.

Pod Wawelem
ul. Św. Gertrudy 26–29; tel: 12 421 2336; www.pod wawelem.eu; daily noon–midnight; €; tram: 3, 6, 8, 10; map p.135 C3

Reminiscent of a Czech beer hall, portions here are obscene, with grilled animals arriving in steel pans and on wooden boards. Evenings get seriously animated, with beer glasses foaming and clinking to the oompah din of the wandering band.

Różowy Słoń
ul. Straszewskiego 24; tel: 12 422 1000; Mon–Sat 9am–8pm, Sun 11am–7pm; €; tram: 2, 3, 4, 8; map p.132 A2

Close to the University, the Pink Elephant is a popular student hangout partly down to the wacky cartoons on the walls and partly thanks to the food, which is basic, albeit nutritious, and, most importantly, as cheap as the proverbial chips.

Prices for an average three-course meal with wine:
€€€€   over 200zł
€€€   100–200zł
€€   50–100zł
€   under 50zł

San Sebastian
ul. Św. Sebastiana 25; tel: 12 429 2476; www.san sebastian.pl; daily 10am–10pm; €€€; tram: 1, 7, 13, 19; map p.135 D2

There's a light, almost Mediterranean style to San Sebastian, a venue whose principal fame owes much to its steaks. Finding a good cow in Poland is hard, finding a chef who can cook one even harder. Here's a place that gets both right, with your meat served precisely as ordered inside golden interiors filled with (fittingly) leather armchairs.

Someplace Else
ul. Powiśle 7; tel: 12 662 1670; www.sheraton.com/krakow; Mon–Thur noon–midnight, Fri–Sat noon–1am; €€€; tram: 1, 2, 6; map p.134 A3

109

Left: an upmarket take on Polish cuisine's staples of game, cabbage and beetroot.

specials, among whose number are found Polish mainstays like stuffed cabbage leaves (gołąbki) and potato pancakes (placki ziemniaczane). Observe the comings and goings on pl. Bohaterów Getta while matronly staff fuss and flap amidst a simple design of kitchen cupboards and frilly lace.

NOWA HUTA
Café Styl
os. Centrum C3; tel: 12 644 2619; daily 9am–11pm; €; tram: 4, 16, 17, 21

At over 50 years old, Café Styl once had its very own statue of Lenin outside. With a few concessions to modernity such as bleeping fruit machines, this is Nowa Huta as it should be sampled, as indeed it should be the food, which is pure canteen quality. The small summer terrace is a great place to rub shoulders with a few of the area's more colourful characters.

Santorini
ul. Bulwarowa 35b; tel: 12 680 5195; www.santorini. krakow.pl; daily 10am–11pm; €€; tram: 4, 16, 17, 21

Supposedly Greek, this hotel restaurant is about as posh as it gets in Nowa Huta. If there's such a thing as three-star white-tablecloth dining then this is it. Steer clear of the international food and head straight for the local dishes.

Right: tuck into the many sweet treats on offer.

To come to Poland and then visit the American-themed sports bar of a five-star hotel seems a waste, but this spot merits attention for reasons aplenty. Boasting Kraków's best burger and excellent fajitas, this is exactly the comfort blanket that's needed if you come across Kraków on a grey, gloomy day. Decor doesn't surprise with its Route 66 signs and photographs of rock gods, but Someplace Else has become a firm and reliable favourite among all those tired of gambling on the humour and skill of local chefs and servers.

Targowy
ul. Daszyńskiego 19; tel: 12 421 1437; Mon–Fri 6am–7pm, Sat–Sun 7am–3pm; €; tram: 1, 11, 14, 22

Just north of Galeria Kazimierz, this gorgeous little gem is about as far removed from its neighbour in terms of style as it gets. A traditional milk bar in a housing-estate setting, don't expect any English once you're over the threshold, but do prepare for honest working-class fare served in an instant for buttons.

PODGÓRZE AND PŁASZÓW
Jadłodajnia Wczoraj i Dzis
pl. Bohaterów Getta 10; tel: 12 346 1428; €; tram: 7, 9, 11, 13; map p.137 E2

Chalked up on the blackboard are the day's

Prices for an average three-course meal with wine:	
€€€€	over 200zł
€€€	100–200zł
€€	50–100zł
€	under 50zł

KATOWICE
Cristallo
ul. Dworcowa 5; tel: 32 782 8209; www.hotel.com.pl; Mon–Fri 5–11pm, Sat–Sun noon–11pm; €€€€

The premium prices are justified in Cristallo, Katowice's principal spot for fine dining. Set under a sloping glass roof, and decorated with parlour palms and industrial finishes, Cristallo's sensational interiors are nearly as good as the food. The cosmopolitan menu includes beautifully presented game as well as seasonal dishes made using the finest locally sourced ingredients.

Zakonnicy
pl. Wolności 6; tel: 32 781 8486; www.zakonnicy.pl; Mon–Fri 9am–10.30pm, Sat–Sun noon–10.30pm; €€

A charming anomaly with a monastic theme and traditional Polish dishes named after saints and sinners.

Why not start with Lucifer Soup, before concluding with a piece of Sister Gwen's Sole? As gimmicks go it's all good fun, with plenty of stained-glass embellishments and even the background sound of chanting monks.

ZAKOPANE
Bąkowo Zohylina
ul. Piłsudskiego 6; tel: 18 206 6216; www.zohylina.pl; daily 1–11.30pm; €€

Taking the Górale cuisine experience to a higher level, this standout restaurant just off the main street manages to combine a traditional mountain style with something altogether more ostentatious. The grilled meats really are outstanding and the service knocks spots off the other eateries hereabouts.

Gubałówka
ul. Gubałówka 2; tel: 18 206 3630; daily 10am–6pm; €

Straight out of The Sound

Several of the parks listed in this book offer excellent opportunities for dining alfresco during the warmer months of the year. In Kraków, both the Botanical Gardens and Błonia come highly recommended, the latter being a particular summer favourite with the locals during the summer. If you're staying in an apartment, making a picnic is easy. If not, then a few shops sell food ready to eat. The best choice of all for picnic food can be found inside the Alma supermarket in Galeria Kazimierz. See also Parks and Gardens, p.100; Shopping, p.115.

of Music, Gubałówka's large interior and even bigger terrace with breathtaking views of the mountains are the places to head year round for classic Górale food with the best scenery in Zakopane. Find it at the top of the funicular railway immediately to the right as you exit at the top.

Salt Mines

An essential ingredient for both preserving and flavouring food, the extraction of rock salt *(halite)*, the raw ingredient used for making the salt found on kitchen tables around the world, dates from at least 8,000 years ago. Formed in huge layers after the evaporation of lakes and seas, rock salt has been mined in Poland since at least the 13th century. Historically an immensely valuable resource (the etymology of the word salary can be traced back to the word salt), two former salt mines close to Kraków are open to the public and are well worth a visit.

WIELICZKA

ul. Daniłowicza 10, Wieliczka; tel: 12 278 7302; www. kopalnia.pl; daily 7.30am– 7.30pm; admission charge

Second only in popularity to Auschwitz as an out-of-town trip from Kraków and a Unesco World Heritage site since 1978, the truly astonishing salt mine in the small town of Wieliczka about 15km (9 miles) attracts an average of a million visitors a year and is, literally, out of this world. The rock salt here is believed to have formed some 15 million years ago and was mined continuously from the 13th century until 2007.

Reaching depths of 327m (1,073ft), the 3.5km (2-mile) tour of the mine complex takes in countless shafts and chambers, one of them large enough to hold a hot-air balloon and most of them full of extraordinary carvings made by the mine's workers over the past several hundred years. Outstanding highlights include the

17th-century Baroque Chapel of St Anthony, and the Chapel of St Kinga, dating from 1896, adorned with scenes from the New Testament carved entirely from salt and lit by huge salt chandeliers hanging from the ceiling.

Tours end with a visit to the mine's underground restaurant 125m (410ft) beneath the surface of the town above and a chance to buy souvenirs in the underground gift shop. The mine also boasts its own brass orchestra, founded 170 years ago, which occasionally plays for tourists and puts on classical concerts. Every New Year, the mine hosts an extraordinary underground party complete with a full orchestra.

The town of Wieliczka itself is a sleepy and rather uneventful settlement of 20,000 people founded in 1290 and with very little else to see. Regular trains and minibuses depart from Kraków throughout the day, taking from between 20 and 40 minutes to make

the journey. Every other business in Kraków now offers organised trips to the mine, although none of them are really worth the extra expense; it is as easy to visit independently. A visit during the peak summer season often involves a lot of waiting. Note that all visitors will need to join a guided tour, which are conducted in a range of languages. The mine is best seen during the quieter parts of the year.

Left: the incredible Chapel of St Kinga at Wieliczka.

make a real day of it would be to hire a car and take in both mines whilst taking the opportunity to explore one or two other local sights. Another 30km (19 miles) in the same direction is the lovely medieval town of Tarnów *(see box)*, with a perfectly preserved Old Town and some really fine examples of local wooden churches.

The same distance again north of Tarnów, the tiny village of Zalipie is renowned for its brightly painted houses. Following on from an older tradition, since 1965 the weekend after the Catholic feast of Corpus Christi has seen 20 or so of the best artists in the village, of whom most are women, paint incredible folk designs on and in their cottages, which are subsequently judged by a panel of experts. Even if a trip during this time isn't possible, the village is an extraordinary sight year-round.

BOCHNIA

ul. Solna 2, Bochnia; tel: 14 615 3636; www.kopalniasoli.pl; several tours daily; admission charge

Europe's oldest salt mine is located in the small town of Bochnia some 40km (25 miles) southeast of Kraków, and despite being much smaller and considerably less impressive than its larger counterpart at Wieliczka, it does feature a few remarkable qualities that more than justify the trip. Established sometime in the 12th century, the Bochnia salt mine reinvented itself in the most interesting manner in 1995 when it became a combined tourist sight and health spa. The entire mine comprises 16 levels going to a depth of about 470m (1,540ft), some of which is open to the public for tours.

Highlights for tourists include an underground café and a small chapel, which, although not as elaborate as the ones at Wieliczka, is still a sight to behold. Perhaps most interestingly, the mine's largest chamber has been converted into a sanatorium where guests can stay and receive a number of treatments for a wide range of physical ailments.

As for Bochnia itself, trains run regularly from Kraków and take about 45 minutes to make the journey. A better option to

Situated about 80km (50 miles) east of Kraków at the crossroads of two ancient trading routes, the medieval town of Tarnów features an immaculately preserved Old Town of outstanding Gothic, Baroque and Renaissance architecture and is well worth considering as a further day trip for those spending a week or more in the area. The first Polish city to declare independence in 1918, Tarnów is rapidly becoming a popular destination for local and international tourists. For more information, see the excellent website at www.go-tarnow.com.

Left: extraordinary salt carvings at Wieliczka.

Shopping

Just over two decades since the demise of communism, Poland's shops are unrecognisable from those of 1989. The shelves are full, the queues are gone and malls have mushroomed like neon toadstools throughout the country. To call Poland a shoppers' paradise would be somewhat extreme, but it can't be denied things have come a long way in the giddy world of consumer culture. Although malls now flourish, just as importantly so do dusty antiques stores, privately run galleries and backstreet oddities. For further shopping listings, *see Food and Drink, p.63, Literature, p.77, Markets, p.78, and Music, p.93.*

ART AND ANTIQUES
Art De&Co
pl. Dominikański 4; tel: 12 423 2246; Mon–Fri 10am–7pm, Sat 10am–4pm; tram: 1, 3, 6, 8; map p.133 C1
A classic Old Town antiques shop crammed to the ceiling with a fascinating wealth of old things, among them paintings, furniture, perfume bottles, plenty of bric-a-brac and some fine original posters.

> People visiting Poland by air from non-EU countries can claim back the VAT they pay on everything they buy that they choose to take out the country when they leave, provided they do so from a shop showing the Tax Free logo. When purchasing goods, ask for a Refund Cheque which can be shown at the customs section of the airport along with a valid receipt and a copy of the buyer's passport. This will get stamped and the VAT can then be claimed in cash or on a credit card at any of the Duty Free shops in the airport. The offer applies to any goods bought within three months of the departure date. For more information see the international Tax Free website at www.globalrefund.com.

FASHION
Reserved
al. Pokoju 44; tel: 12 684 0398; www.reserved.pl; Mon–Sat 10am–9pm, Sun 10am–8pm; tram: 1, 14, 22
A hugely successful, predominantly youthful Polish fashion chain with outlets around the country and abroad, this is the best of its local shops. Find it inside the Kraków Plaza shopping centre.

Vistula
ul. Piwna 24; tel: 12 656 2086; www.vistula.pl; Mon–Fri 10am–9pm, Sat 10am–2pm; tram: 7, 9, 11, 13; map p.137 E2
A long-established Kraków fashion house born from the city's communist-era sweatshops and now completely reinvented as a serious and stylish operation.

Zebra
ul. Szczepańska 7; tel: 12 422 4605; www.zebra-buty.pl;

Above: religious prints are a fittingly Krakovian souvenir.

Mon–Fri 10am–7pm; Sat 10am–4pm; tram: 2, 3, 4, 12; map p.132 B3
Another successful Polish company, this one dealing in a good range of footwear for everyone.

PHOTOGRAPHY
Fotojoker
ul. Pawia 5; tel: 12 433 0122; www.fotojoker.pl; Mon–Sat 9am–10pm, Sun 10am–9pm; tram: 2, 4, 7, 10; map p.133 E4
The Old Town has several small photographic shops that tend to concentrate mostly on services. This place, inside the massive

Left: all manner of antique bells for sale in Kazimierz.

Despite the large tract of land between Kraków and the sea, amber *(bursztyn)* plays a significant part in the commercial life of the city. As with all amber, be careful of cheap imitations, often sold from small outdoor stalls in Old Town. The best places to look for quality are the better class of jewellers and the traders operating inside the Cloth Hall.

Galeria Krakowska, provides all the services required for analogue and digital photographs and also sells a wide range of digital compact cameras and dSLRs. If you can't find it here, try the large Saturn electrical store in the same building.

SHOPPING MALLS
Galeria Kazimierz
ul. Podgórska 34; tel: 12 433 0101; www.galeriakaz imierz.pl; Mon–Sat 10am–10pm, Sun 10am–8pm; tram: 7, 9, 11, 13
The older of the city's two most famous shopping malls, Galeria Kazimierz features two floors of shopping with stores including a few household names such as C&A and Sony. Although concentrating mostly on fashion and footwear, there are a few other surprises here, among them the Alma supermarket, arguably the best supermarket in the

city. Upstairs is an area where young people gather to play board games, a multi-screen cinema and a fairly decent food hall with the compulsory McDonald's, as well as a few more interesting choices including North Fish, which serves Polish versions of the classic fish and chips meal.

Galeria Krakowska
ul. Pawia 5; tel: 12 428 9900; www.galeria-krakowska.pl; Mon–Sat 9am–10pm, Sun

10am–9pm; tram: 2, 4, 7, 10; map p.133 E4
With no less than three floors of retail and restaurants, Galeria Krakowska is the closest of its type to the Old Town and can sell you just about anything you ever needed and more besides. Surplus to the endless rows of fashion outlets are a large Carrefour supermarket, a good chemist shop and representatives of all three Polish mobile-phone operators. The downstairs tunnel that connects the mall with the train station next door is worth finding. Lined down one side are countless kiosks selling

Right: traditional fashion designs on offer.

Visitors looking for something old and unusual to take home with them when they leave should take advantage of the growing number of antiques and bric-a-brac shops springing up all over Kazimierz.

Found mostly in the area around Plac Nowy, these fascinating places are generally crammed with goods spilling out onto the street and sell everything from broken dolls to original artwork to communist-era children's toys and much more besides. Haggling at all places is considered fair game.

second-hand books and dirt-cheap, if slightly dubious, DVDs.

SPECIALITY SHOPS
Arkos

pl. Mariacki 5; 12 421 8661; Mon–Fri 10am–6pm, Sat 10am–2pm; tram: 1, 3, 6, 8; map p.133 C2

Where else in staunchly Catholic Poland would you find not one but a row of shops selling religious items for home and/or church use. Arkos, the end one on the corner by St Mary's Basilica, is one of the largest and the best of the bunch. Inside you'll find an extraordinary collection of things from chalices to

complete priest outfits to the more downmarket, but equally intriguing, Pope John Paul II tea trays. One of the city's more bizarre shops and a good source of novelty gifts and souvenirs.

Kapelusze Czapki

ul. Krakowska 35a; tel: 12 430 6114; www.czapki chorazy.prv.pl; Mon–Fri 10am–6pm, Sat 10am–2pm; tram: 3, 6, 8, 10; map p.136 B3

Opened not long after independence by a gentleman whose family comes from a long line of milliners, this Kazimierz curiosity celebrates a country where hats still pack a punch, especially among the older generation. Making both civilian and military headgear for gentlemen, the shop specialises mostly in caps and trilbies, and will make anything required from any material that can be applied to make a hat.

SPORT AND LEISURE
White Sports

al. 3 Maja 5; tel: 12 634 5122; www.whitesports.pl; Mon–Fri 10am–6pm, Sat 10am–2pm; tram: 15, 18

A decent range of sports gear and clothing plus help at hand for visitors

who suddenly find themselves with a broken tennis racquet in need of emergency repairs. Also a small stock of wintersports equipment for those moving on to Zakopane to take advantage of the ski slopes.

STATIONERY
EMPiK Megastore

Rynek Główny 5; tel: 12 429 4162; www.empik.com; daily 9am–10pm; tram: 1, 3, 6, 8; map p.132 C2

With over 60 years in the business, this one-time state-owned national chain has stores all over the country, including three large ones in Kraków (the other two being inside Galeria Kazimierz and Galeria Krakowska, see p.115). On several floors, EMPiK sells not only a wide range of stationery but cameras, art supplies, iPods, books including guidebooks and novels in English, maps, music CDs and an excellent range of DVDs.

Of the last two, as well as plenty of Western classics there's also arguably the city's best choice of local talents, from rack-loads of CDs by the city's recently expired crooner,

Above: glassware and amber for sale.

Marek Grechuta, who is well worth investigating, to an ever-increasing range of box sets of Polish feature films and documentaries, many of them with English subtitles. An indispensable store and highly recommended.

KATOWICE
Kamelia
ul. Stawowa 6; tel: 32 259 8995; Mon–Fri 10am–6pm, Sat 10am–2pm, Sun 10am–1pm
Flower shops and stalls are everywhere in Poland, and finding one should never be much of a challenge. Some, including this small shop close to the train station, can also deliver. This one is also an Interflora agent.

Silesia City Center
ul. Chorzowska 107; tel: 32 605 0000; www.silesiacitycenter. com.pl; Sat–Thur 10am–9pm, Fri 10am–10pm
On the main tram route to Chorzów on the site of an old coal mine, just about the only thing you can't

Left: the vast Galeria Krakowska *(see p.115).*

get in Silesia City Center is a guided tour, which is a pity because it's not that hard to get completely lost inside the maze of aisles that make up this vast shopping mall. As well as an enormous Tesco supermarket the size of a football field, the mall comes with the usual collection of fashion outlets, a decent EMPiK store *(see opposite)* and a food court bigger than many town squares. There's also a microbrewery serving good beer and recommended German sausages, a multi-screen cinema and, in a separate building outside, a chapel inside the mine's former pit-shaft machine room.

ZAKOPANE
Galeria M. Jędrysiak
ul. Droga na Gubałówkę 2; tel: 18 201 3546
Found at the main entrance to Zakopane's sprawling outdoor market, this small gallery-shop sells local artworks of all persuasions, from a handful of paintings of a distinctly dubious taste to some excellent examples

of the local speciality glass paintings covered in a range of colourful folk-art motifs. Note that in true Zakopane style, opening hours are relaxed to say the least.

Should you find yourself in need of giving flowers *(kwiaty)* to somebody in Poland for whatever reason, it's worth bearing in mind that there are a number of complicated rules and procedures that need to be followed in order to not offend. With the exception of solemn occasions, always give an odd number of flowers or stems, although be warned that with the exception of a single rose given for romantic reasons, giving just one flower is looked upon as a cruel and miserly act. Chrysanthemums and lilies, as lovely as they are, are almost universally reserved for the cemetery, so be careful not to fall into that particularly embarrassing trap. Yellow flowers should be generally avoided, as indeed should red carnations, a still potent symbol of communism. If in doubt, ask a local for guidance.

Sports

Kraków may not be a sporting hotbed, but it should be pointed out that the region's contribution to the world of sport is not quite as inconsequential as one may first believe. Wisła Kraków have emerged as the dominant force in Polish football, whilst local-born Formula 1 driver Robert Kubica and tennis player Agnieszka Radwańska have made impressive strides in their chosen fields. For the more active visitor, the city now offers a number of cycle paths, a newfound nouveau riche appreciation of golf and several skiing options on the nearby slopes of Zakopane, a recent nominee to host the Winter Olympics.

CYCLING

Kraków has made impressive strides to make the city bike-friendly in recent years, adding cycle lanes and introducing community-conscious bike-rental schemes. Always be on guard for cars in cycle lanes, and note that the tough drink-driving laws are applied identically to drunk cyclists.

BikeOne

www.bikeone.pl
With 16 automated rental points throughout the city, BikeOne is a city initiative to encourage cycling, with trips of less than 20 minutes free of charge and those between 20 minutes and one hour charged at just 1.20zł. To take advantage of this you'll need to register via the (Polish-language) website, leave a 120zł deposit through your credit card and then note the ID and PIN number you're issued. The most visible rental points are pl. Wyszystich Świętich and at pl. Bernardyński by Wawel.

Dwa Kola

ul. Józefa 5; tel: 12 421 5785; www.dwakola.internetdsl.pl; Mon–Fri 10am–6pm, Sat 10am–2pm; tram: 7, 9, 11, 13; map p.136 C4
Mountain and city bikes available, deposit and photographic ID required.

Jordan

ul. Szeroka 2; tel: 12 429 1374; www.jarden.pl; Mon–Fri 9am–6pm, Sat–Sun 10am–6pm; tram: 7, 9, 11, 13; map p.135 E2
A range of bikes in tip-top condition. Deposit and photographic ID required.

FOOTBALL

While hooliganism is on the wane, it still rears its head at times, and casual fans are advised to avoid hairy moments by buying the most expensive seats. Surprisingly, given its transport links and choice of hotels, Kraków was left off the list of Euro 2012 host cities.

Wisła Kraków

ul. Reymonta 22; www.wisla.krakow.pl; tram: 2, 3, 8, 15
With seven league titles in

Every now and again visitors will find the city locked down as locals gather round televisions to follow Robert Kubica's or Agnieszka Radwańska's sporting fortunes. The hotly rated Kubica became Poland's first ever representative in Formula 1 in 2006, sealing his maiden first-place finish in the 2008 Canadian Grand Prix. From 2010, the former BMW Sauber driver will be appearing in the colours of Renault. Radwańska, meanwhile, is seen as Poland's great tennis hope, winning Junior Wimbledon in 2005 and becoming only the second Polish female to reach a Grand Slam quarter final since turning pro.

the last 10 years, no other team in Poland has come close to matching the recent success of Wisła Kraków, and while European success remains elusive, going to a match is a colourful and cheap outing.

Cracovia

ul. Kałuży 1; www.cracovia.pl; tram: 2, 3, 8, 15
Kraków's other side have a

Left: a packed-out Cracovia football stadium.

SKIING

Zakopane is Poland's premier ski resort, and the Tatra mountains which loom in the background are frequently home to international ski-jumping events. Boast knowledge of the sport by professing admiration of Adam Małysz, a Wisła-born jumper who won the World Cup an impressive four times. The 1,985m (6,512ft) Kasprowy Wierch is regarded as the best, even if access to the top is reached by a cable car built in the 1930s. Nosal, Gubałówka and Białka are also popular, very much so in fact, so expect lengthy queues for both ski rental and lifts.

Sukces

ul. Nowotarska 39; tel: 18 200 0231; daily 9am–6pm; www.ski-sukces.zakopane.pl
Ski and snowboard rentals, as well as tuition available.

SWIMMING

Kryspinów Lagoon

Liszki; tel: 12 292 7553; www.kryspinow.com.pl; summer daily 8am–10pm; admission charge; tram: 1,2, 6
Locals make their way to the artificial beach here, a 12km (7½-mile) journey from the centre. Attractions here include guarded waters, a 'rope park' for climbing between trees, windsurfing and zorbing.

Wodny Park

ul. Dobrego Pasterza 126; tel: 12 616 3190; www.parkwodny.pl; daily 8am–10pm; admission charge
A modern aqua park with slides, wave machines, spa and a wellness centre.

long and distinguished history, and are recognised as the oldest professional club in Poland. Pope John Paul II was an avid fan, and whilst their fans are a little better behaved than their local rivals the derby game, known as The Holy War, sees thugs from both sides emerging from the woodwork. Success has largely avoided Cracovia and crowds are entertained in a ramshackle stadium.

GOLF

A post-Iron Curtain desire to follow Western culture has seen the wealthier Krakovian adopt golf, and today there's a number of country clubs and driving ranges within easy distance of the city centre. Whilst Poland has yet to provide the world with a professional player of note, enthusiasm for the amateur game continues to grow at a rapid rate.

Kraków Valley

ul. Pacziółtowice 328; tel: 12 258 6000; www.krakow-valley.com
Aside from an 18-hole course, this complex touts a driving range, putting green, 16-room hotel and diversions that include shooting range, horse riding, sledging and even a 650m (2,133ft) ski slope.

Royal Kraków Golf and Country Club

ul. Ochmanów 124; tel: 12 281 9170; www.krakowgolf.cal.pl
A nine-hole golf course set 18km (11 miles) east of downtown Kraków. Also includes indoor driving ranges.

Below: fun in the snow at Zakopane.

119

Theatre

It's common to hear the term 'Poland's cultural capital' applied to Kraków, and it's a claim given credence by a particularly rich and varied theatre scene. Theatre has enjoyed an elevated status in the city for over two centuries, with a history that can be traced back to when the Stary Teatr first opened its doors towards the end of the 18th century. Kraków's theatres enjoy a noble and distinguished reputation across Europe. With everything from large-scale, state-funded stage companies to privately run experimental theatres, the city offers a diverse number of productions. Note that the majority of performances will be in Polish.

POLISH THEATRE

It's no surprise to learn that Polish drama enjoyed its heyday in the 19th century, when the country was effectively wiped off the map for the best part of the century. During this time feelings of nationhood were expressed in the form of two crushed armed uprisings, as well as passively by way of the arts. Themes of betrayal, oppression and patriotism feature heavily in the works of the era, which were utilised as the mouthpiece of the Polish people.

Prominent playwrights and dramatists of the time included **Michał Bałucki** (1837–1901), **Juliusz Słowacki** (1809–49), best known for his tragedy *Lilla Weneda*, comedy writer **Aleksander Fredro** (1793–1876) and **Cyprian Norwid** (1821–83). However, few are celebrated locally as much as Kraków-born **Stanisław Wyspiański** (1869–1907), the author of acclaimed dramas such as *Noc Listopadowa* (November Night), *Klątwa* (The

Above: the Groteska-organised Great Dragon Parade.

Curse) and *Wesele* (The Wedding). Regarded as one of the defining works of Polish drama, *Wesele* tells the epic story of an aristocratic Kraków marriage set to a background of political upheaval. It's been twice turned into film, first by Andrzej Wajda, and more recently by Wojtek Smarzowski, and continues to be an audience favourite in theatres across the nation.

THEATRES
Groteska
ul. Skarbowa 2; tel: 12 633 4822; www.groteska.pl; box office: Mon–Fri 8am–noon, 3–5pm, Sat–Sun one hour before performances; tram: 4, 8, 12, 13

A spectacular puppet theatre which has been mounting shows since 1945, although best known for organising Kraków's annual Great Dragon Parade. While performances tend to be in Polish only, it is easy to follow the action, and you'll find events being enjoyed by an audience of children of all nationalities. Shows aimed at a more adult crowd, featuring Brecht, Bulgakov and Voltaire and sinister-looking puppets, are also frequently staged. SEE ALSO FESTIVALS, P.56

Łaźnia Nowa Teatr
ul. os. Szkolne 25, Nowa Huta; tel: 12 425 0320; www.laznia nowa.pl; box office: Mon–Fri 9am–4.30pm; tram: 4, 16, 21, 22

With a defiantly bohemian attitude to drama, this young theatre troupe's performances have included such oddities as a fox, a bishop and a cockerel discussing the morality of the 20th century, with shows

Left: Aleksander Fredro was a significant Polish playwright.

Jerzy Fedorowicz hit the headlines for using rival local hooligans in his take on *Romeo and Juliet*. This is a theatre troupe that merits the hype.

Teatr Mumerus
ul. Kanonicza 1; tel: 12 645 9273; www.mumerus.net; tram: 3, 6, 8, 10; map p.134 C4
Even in a city not short on alternative culture, this offers something different. The listed venue aside, this group can be found performing their peculiar brand of theatre on the streets, in pub cellars and inside abandoned factories. The repertoire includes quirky takes on Kafka and Swift, and can be enjoyed with no prior knowledge of Polish.

Teatr Nowy
ul. Gazowa 21; tel: 12 790 451322; www.teatrnowy.com.pl; box office: two hours before performances; tram: 7, 9, 11, 13; map p.137 C3
The primary aim of this group is to give aspiring actors a springboard to fame, as well as introducing contemporary European theatre to all.

For the lucky few staying in style, a whispered word with the concierge will prove enough to learn what's on and where. Generally speaking, tickets can also be procured this way. Others looking to keep abreast of latest events should consult the internet. To this end, www.krakow-info.com, www.e-teatr.pl and http://krakow.inyourpocket.com should all prove sufficient.

performed by amateur actors recruited from the neighbouring tower blocks. That a communist-age Polish Fiat hangs from the ceiling of this industrial space should come as no shock.

Stary Teatr
ul. Jagiellońska 5; tel: 12 422 8566; www.stary-teatr.pl; box office: Tue–Sat 10am–1pm, 5–7pm; tram: 4, 8, 13, 14; map p.132 B3
With origins dating back to 1781, the Stary Teatr can count itself as the longest-operating Polish theatre group. Strict censorship in the immediate post-war

years did little to dent the theatre's popularity; it emerged as one of the leading stage companies and has continued to grow in prominence, with appearances by luminaries such as Peter Brook, Robert Ciulli and Czesław Miłosz and modern interpretations of classics such as *Faust*, *The Cherry Orchard* and *The Master and Margarita*.

Teatr Ludowy
ul. os. Teatralne 34, Nowa Huta; tel: 12 680 2100; www.ludowy.pl; box office: Tue–Fri 1–6pm, Sat 3–6pm, Sun two hours before performance; tram: 1, 5
Currently under the guiding hand of director Jacek Strama, the Teatr Ludowy is known as a ground breaker. Since its inception in 1955, this Socialist Realist masterpiece has been the stage for avant-garde works that have proved as thought-provoking as they are surreal. Józef Szajna, director from 1963–6, wove his Auschwitz experiences into productions of Shakespeare, while more recently,

Below: the venerable Art Nouveau Stary Teatr building.

Transport

Kraków's geographical positioning, as well as its ever-growing popularity as a holiday destination, means that it enjoys excellent rail and air connections with the rest of Europe. Polish roads, however, remain a horror story, and even though EU funding has gone some way to changing this, it'll still be a while before driving here is recommended. Kraków itself proves exceptionally easy to get around. Most of the major sights are within walking distance, and those that aren't can be accessed by a public transport system that's among the most user-friendly in Poland.

GETTING THERE

BY AIR

Kraków
John Paul II Kraków
Balice Airport
(www.krakowairport.pl) lies 17km (11 miles) west of the city centre and is at the time of writing used by 20 airlines, including Aer Lingus, BA, easyJet, Lufthansa, Ryanair and the Polish national airline, LOT. Destinations include Birmingham, Bristol, East Midlands, Liverpool and London (Gatwick, Luton and Stansted) in the UK, Chicago and Warsaw, of which the latter uses the

The **Kraków Tourist Card** is ideal if you intend to do a lot of travelling around the city on public transport. Available for 50–65zł, these not only give you free travel for 2–3 days, but also free entry to most museums, and discounts in bars and restaurants. Check www.krakowcard.com for further details. *See also Museums and Galleries, p.83.*

Above: Kraków's bus network is excellent.

new domestic terminal.
 Taxis stand outside the international terminal and will charge anything from 65zł upwards to get to the centre. Note that prices go up by 50 percent after 10pm, and it's not uncommon for foreigners to be scammed. Cut out any margin for disaster by agreeing on a price beforehand. Alternatively, and easiest of all, board the free bus that runs between both terminals and the nearby train station, where regular connections zip back and forth to Kraków Główny (*see*

opposite) in about 15 minutes. Tickets are available from the conductor on board and are currently priced at 8zł.

Katowice
Katowice International
Airport (www.katowice-airport.com) can be found 34km (21 miles) north of Katowice, and touts connections to 29 destinations including Birmingham, Cork, Doncaster/Sheffield, Dublin, Liverpool and London (Luton and Stansted). Carriers using the airport include LOT, Lufthansa, Ryanair and Wizz. Airport buses run to Katowice train station and cost 20zł. Wizz organises buses that go to central Katowice (25zł) and Kraków bus station (50zł), with pre-booking an option when buying your flight ticket.

BY RAIL

Kraków
With direct and daily connections with Berlin, Budapest and Prague, it's no surprise to find many

Left: a train makes its way to Kraków Główny.

the city, with a number of trains running straight to Kraków. Allow approximately 90 minutes for journey time.

Zakopane

A number of trains run from Kraków to Zakopane, with the journey taking approximately three and a half hours. On the whole, traffic disasters permitting, buses prove not just cheaper but faster.

BY ROAD

Car

The perilous state of Polish roads, not to mention the kamikaze attitudes of the country's drivers, makes arriving by car the least advisable option. Speed limits, frequently flouted by locals, stand at 50kph (31mph) in built-up areas, 90kph (56mph) on country roads, 110kph (68mph) on dual carriageways and 130kph (80mph) on motorways. Headlights should be kept on at all times, and drivers should carry their licence and passport.

Mobile-phone use while driving is banned, and strict

Below: a tram trundles through the city.

Ever since the backpacker boom, stories have abounded regarding the safety of the overnight trains which connect Kraków to Berlin, Budapest and Prague. Incidences and subsequent scare stories of gassings and violence were frequent, and while these reports have subsided somewhat, be on the safe side by booking into a sleeping wagon. All of these come with locked compartments and their own personal guard.

continental travellers, especially those tottering under the weight of backpacks, choosing to arrive by rail. Domestically, scores of trains run hourly between Kraków and Warsaw, with many of these continuing the length of the country and terminating up in the port city of Gdynia.

Arrivals (*przyjazdy*) are marked in white, departures (*odjazdy*) in yellow, with domestic tickets available in any one of the scores of windows marked *bilety*. Note that domestic tickets can also be pur-

chased on board from the conductor for a token extra fee. International tickets can be procured from windows 9 and 10 in the main hall. For up-to-the-minute schedules, consult www.pkp.pl. Polish trains are in the process of being upgraded, and as such travellers can expect anything from hi-tech Western efforts to pootling remnants from the Iron Curtain. While Kraków has many train stations, pretty much the only one you'll be needing or stopping at will be the principal one, **Kraków Główny**. Old Town lies a few minutes southwest. Simply cross the plaza by Galeria Krakowska, and follow the herd as they disappear through the underpass.

Those laden with luggage will find (reputable) taxis waiting on the rooftop car park. Access is via the stairs found on each platform (*peron*).

Katowice

Katowice's grim train station is right in the heart of

Above: Kraków is very suitable for cycling *(see Sports, p.118).*

drink-driving laws mean that even one unit of alcohol will be seen as too much. Expect heavy traffic on entering Kraków, as well as a complex one-way system that still baffles the locals. Note that many Polish drivers ignore red lights and zebra crossings, whilst other common hazards adding to the white-knuckle experience include horse-drawn carriages ferrying tourists to and fro.

Katowice

The A4 connecting Katowice to Kraków is one of Poland's best roads, with a 6.50zł toll in place at either end for its use. The 75km (47-mile) journey is straightforward enough,

Plain-clothes ticket inspectors regularly stalk the lines, making good sport of catching foreigners who've failed to validate their ticket. Penalties are fixed at 100zł for no valid ticket and 75zł for no valid ID if travelling as a child or student. Be warned, feigning a lack of funds will result in two outcomes depending on the mood of the conductor. Either a stern telling off and nothing worse, or the summoning of the police and a night in the cells.

and drivers heading to Kraków centre should keep their eyes peeled for signs pointing to *centrum*.

Zakopane

Drivers heading to Zakopane will need to take the southbound E77 before moving onto road number 47. The 110km (68-mile) journey is clearly signposted throughout, with the slow speed of traffic allowing little opportunity to miss your mark. The E77 is currently being upgraded and traffic is subject to delays.

BY BUS

Those who choose to arrive by long-distance bus will find Kraków to be the owner of a sparkling new bus station set just east of the train station. Found on ul. Bosacka 18, the two-floor **Dworzec Autobusowy** has frequent buses running to Oświęcim (Auschwitz), Ojców National Park, Wieliczka salt mine and Zakopane. Numerous international routes also exist, including regular connections from Amsterdam, Brussels, Lvov, Kiev, Paris and Rome. Tickets for international destinations can be purchased from the top-

floor station building at the point marked *Kasa Między-naradowa* (daily 9am–5pm). For further details including timetables, check www.rda.krakow.pl.

SEE ALSO AUSCHWITZ, P.28; SALT MINES, P.112

Katowice

Katowice's bus station can be found in the centre of town at ul. Skargi 1 (www.pkskatowice.internetdsl. pl). Buses to and from Kraków also depart from the stops found directly outside the main entrance to the train station.

Zakopane

Buses depart from Kraków's bus station and take around two hours to make the journey. Taxis stand by at all hours, although the main high street, ul. Krupówki, can be reached by following ul. Kościuszki on foot in a southwesterly direction for approximately 10 minutes.

GETTING AROUND

BY BUS AND TRAM

Visitors will find Kraków has an excellent public transport network, albeit one that's constantly being tampered with. Route changes and line works have become commonplace over

Poland is one of Europe's leaders in road fatalities, with one reason being a road system that's yet to embrace separate lanes for cars heading in one particular direction. Many of the roads in Poland are two-lane affairs, meaning that overtaking is done by straying into the lane set aside for oncoming traffic.

Above: driving a horse-drawn carriage through the Old Town.

commonplace over the last few years, resulting in no end of confusion for locals and visitors alike. Latest tram and bus maps can be found on the municipal transport company website at www.mpk.krakow.pl. There's no English-language option on the website, so instead point to the link that declares *Mapki Komunikacyjne*.

Trams, some cutting-edge Western models, other rusting communist leftovers, circle Old Town as well as firing off in all directions required by tourists including Kazimierz, Podgórze and Płaszów. Tickets *(bilety)* are valid for both trams and buses and can be bought from the little newspaper kiosks lining the streets, directly from the driver (exact change) or from the little machines now found at the newer stops or actually in the newer trams.

Single-use tickets *(bilet normalny)* cost 2.50zł, one-hour tickets (with which it's possible to switch trams) 3.10zł, and one-day tickets 10.40zł. Two-, three- and seven-day passes are also available for 18.80zł, 25zł and 38zł. Discounts are available for students and children, although photographic ID will usually be required if you find yourself stopped by a conductor. It's vital you validate your ticket on boarding, otherwise you'll find yourself facing an on-the-spot fine if caught by a conductor *(see box, opposite)*. Avoid such a fate by stamping your ticket in one of the little box contraptions by the doors. If in doubt, look and learn from the locals. Trams tend to operate from around 5am to 11pm, after which night buses zip around the city sallying partygoers from pub to club to bed.

BY TAXI

The sheer number of tourists walking around with money to spare has led to a rise in fly-by-night cabbies looking for an easy mark. Avoiding being scammed is simple, and involves nothing harder than looking out

for clearly marked cabs with fares written in the window. Make sure the meter is on and if in doubt arrange a fee beforehand or at least enquire as to the approximate price.

Bartenders, concierges and waiting staff will also be happy to order you a taxi from a reputable company. By and large taxis charge an initial fee of around 5–7zł, then 2.30zł or thereabouts for every kilometre after. Don't necessarily expect taxis standing outside five-star hotels to be the cheapest, and ignore anyone who approaches you to offer the deal of your life in the arrivals halls at the airport. Companies with a good reputation include the following, of which most have an English-speaking switchboard operator.

Barbakan
Tel: 12 96 61

City
Tel: 12 96 21

Euro
Tel: 12 96 64

Radio
Tel: 12 91 91

Tele Taxi
Tel: 12 96 26

Left: taxis ply their trade.

125

Walks and Tours

Kraków can be seen from a hot-air balloon, a horse and carriage, bicycle and even a golf buggy. All fun without a doubt, but none of them a patch on seeing the city at your own pace. It's on foot that Kraków reveals her finer details, from hidden courtyards to secret cellars. It's also whilst walking that the lives of three of her more illustrious former habitants come to life. Oskar Schindler, immortalised as the Good Nazi, Kraków's artistic genius, Stanisław Wyspiański, and the city's religious icon, Pope John Paul II. Their footsteps can be followed and their Kraków discovered using the routes detailed below.

RECOMMENDED WALKS
John Paul II's Kraków
Start: ul. Tyniecka 10; bus: 112, 162
End: Basilica of St Francis on ul. Franciszkańska 3; tram: 2, 3, 4, 8; map p.132 B1
Born in Wadowice, some 50km (31 miles) to the southwest of Kraków, Karol Wojtyła (1920–2005), better known to the world as Pope John Paul II, moved to the city when he

Two recommended places for two very different but equally superb views of the city are the tower at **St Mary's Basilica** (see Churches and Synagogues, p.42), which is only open during the summer and requires a good bit of energy to reach the top, and **Panorama**, a restaurant, bar and club on the top floor of the Jublilat shopping centre at ul. Zwierzyniecka 50 (www.panoramaklub.eu). The latter isn't going to win any awards for outstanding food or service in the near future, but the view of Wawel and the river from the terrace is easily one of the best in town.

was 18 years old and would go on to spend a considerable part of the next four decades in Kraków. Pope-related sights are numerous, and visitors following in his footsteps should start their trail in the district of Dębniki south of the river and just west of Wawel.

Wojtyła first took lodgings at ul. Tyniecka 10 where a plaque marks his presence, and when he wasn't breaking rocks under Nazi guard in the Zakrzówek Quarry nearby, he spent his wartime years diligently studying in his basement apartment. He attended daily worship in the **Church of St Stanisław Kostka** (ul. Konfederacka 6), and it was here that he took his second Mass two days after being ordained on 1 November, 1946. Visit the site of his first, conducted the day before, by crossing the river and heading to the **Crypt of St Leonard** underneath **Wawel Cathedral**.

Above: a detail on an ul. Grodzka building.

Walk to ul. Kanonicza 19 for the Holy Grail of papal tourism, none other than the **Archdiocesan Museum** (see Museums and Galleries, p.82). Wojtyła resided here from 1951 to 1958, and then in the adjoining building until 1963. Personal effects such as gifts received from world leaders are today on view. Directly opposite at number 18 is the temporary HQ of the **John Paul II Center**, a theological

Left: ul. Kanonicza, where Pope John Paul II once lived.

property forcibly requisitioned from its Jewish owners). Spielberg shot most of the Ghetto scenes in Kazimierz using ul. Szeroka in place of pl. Bohaterów Getta, and the courtyard on ul. Józefa 12 for the scene where a mother desperately hides her daughter. Both will look familiar to those who have seen the film.

For sights of genuine Schindler interest, cross to Podgórze to reach ul. Józefińska 2, formerly Pfefferberg's house, and then continue on to pl. Bohaterów Getta to visit the Pharmacy Under the Eagle, now the **Museum of National Remembrance** *(see Museums and Galleries, p.88)*. Schindler's one-time factory, on ul. Lipowa 4 *(see Museums and Galleries, p.89)*, is also open to visitors, although quite what condition you'll find it in is open to question. At the time of writing all that was open was a photographic display, the stairwell leading to Schindler's office and a small screen projecting

centre which will eventually be relocated to Podgórze and has a few items of interest to visitors, including a bizarre machine in the entrance hall that mints your very own Pope John Paul II coin at the press of a button.

In the 15 years leading up to his papal appointment in 1978, Wojtyła resided in the Bishop's Palace next to the **Basilica of St Francis of Assisi** on ul. Franciszkańska 3 *(see Churches and Synagogues, p.43)*, and could often be found conversing with followers from his window, a practice he resumed when he stayed here during his last couple of visits to Kraków. A statue honours him in the courtyard. During these landmark visits he said Mass at huge events held on the Błonia *(see Parks and Gardens, p.100)*.

Schindler's Kraków
Start: ul. Grodzka 48; tram: 2, 3, 4, 8; map p.134 C4
End: Liban Quarry on ul. Za Torem; tram: 3, 6, 9, 13

Immortalised in the cinematic and literary works of Steven Spielberg and Thomas Keneally, Oskar Schindler (1908–74), the Nazi Party member credited with saving approximately 1,200 Jews during World War II, will for ever be linked with the city of Kraków. It's on ul. Grodzka 48, in his mother's house, that key character Leopold Pfefferberg first met Schindler, who himself didn't live far away, choosing to take quarters in the top-floor flat on ul. Starszewskiego 7 (a

Below: the walls of the former Ghetto.

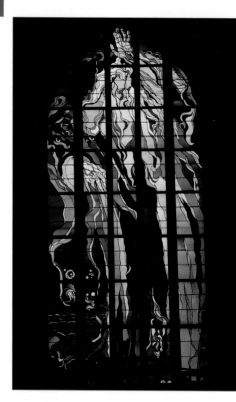

End: Pauline Church, ul. Skałeczna; tram: 18, 19, 22; map p.136 A3

For someone who lived such a short and, towards the end, tragic life, Kraków-born-and-bred Stanisław Wyspiański (1869–1907) accomplished great success as an architect, painter, playwright and poet. His fierce patriotism, religious beliefs and prolific activity in the world of the applied arts left the city with not only someone to be immensely proud of but also a legacy of work scattered around available to anyone prepared to put in a bit of legwork. For those not too familiar with the artist, the logical place to begin is in the museum that bears his name *(see Museums and Galleries, p.85)*. Showcasing not only the artist's vision of tradition, modernity and a distinctively Polish influence, the museum also goes into detail about his private life and offers the perfect primer for a Wyspiański-related tour of the city.

Also in the Old Town are the early polychrome and stained-glass windows in **St Mary's Basilica** *(see Churches and Synagogues, p.42)* the young Wyspiański worked on whilst still a student in 1889. The other church he contributed to, the **Basilica of St Francis of Assisi** *(see Churches and Synagogues, p.43)*, has stained-glass windows dating from between 1895 and 1904 that caused a controversy when they first appeared. Both of these are within easy walking

survivor testimonies. Head out of the factory and to ul. Lwowska where, just before the intersection with ul. Na Zjeżdzie, a plaque marks a remaining piece of the Ghetto Wall.

Close by, accessed by ul. Rękawka, lies St Benedict's, an imperial Austrian fort that today stands largely in ruins. It's around here, while riding on horseback, that Schindler first noticed the 'girl in the red dress', a pivotal moment which would, at least so the legend goes, change his philosophy for ever. Finally, fans of the film can finish their Schindler tour by visiting the now rotting reconstruction that Spielberg built of **Płaszów Concentration Camp**. Find the haunting remains of fences and pathways in the Liban Quarry on ul. Za Torem.
SEE ALSO FILM, P.58

Wyspiański's Kraków
Start: Wyspiański Museum, ul. Szczepańska 11; tram: 2, 3, 4, 12; map p.132 B3

If you have procured yourself a bicycle, a pleasant ride is the route from Wawel to the top of the Piłsudski Mound for unbeatable views of the city.
For something a little less strenuous, cycle to Las Wolski in the west, a scenic forest and a favourite with local cyclists.
See also Sports, p.118.

For the most varied and inclusive tour of Nowa Huta, pick up the free English leaflet at the tourist information centre in Nowa Huta *(see p.19)* which features a specially designed walk to several intriguing local sights, complete with an easy-to-follow map.

distance of the Wyspiański Museum and can be visited in either order before heading east to the **Pollera** hotel (ul. Szpitalna 30), whose grand and recently restored staircase features a quintessential piece of Wyspiański stained glass in one of the windows.

Just east of Old Town at ul. Radziwiłłowska 4 is the **Medical Society Building**, which is usually locked but can be got inside with a confident knock on the front door and a suitable smile. As well as the truly remarkable *Apollo*, completed in 1904 and the last major piece of stained glass to be completed by the artist before he died, the balustrades in the stairwell where the windows are located feature original ornate metal decoration which is also his work.

Over on the other side of town, in front of the **National Museum of Art** (al. 3 Maja 1; *see Museums and Galleries, p.88*) is the surprisingly grey and somewhat austere **Wyspiański Monument**. Unveiled on 28 November 1982 on the 75th anniversary of the artist's death and, strangely perhaps, during the middle of Jaruzelski's martial law, the monument features characters from some of

Wyspiański's best-known plays around the base with the author dressed in a cape on the top. It took no less than five years, several competitions and around 80 unsuccessful designs to realise. The final winner was the Kraków-educated sculptor Marian Konieczny (born 1930), with money for the statue coming from both state and private donation.

After a prolonged period of deteriorating health, Stanisław Wyspiański died of syphilis. His body lies in an extraordinary-looking sarcophagus in the crypt of the **Pauline Church** *(see Churches and Synagogues, p.47)* in Kazimierz.

GUIDED TOURS

Just about every cupboard in Kraków conceals at least one person working in the guided tour industry, making choosing the right one far from simple. Avoid the old men offering tours outside the train station to supplement their pensions and go for something slightly more sophisti-

cated. Ask at hotel reception for a list of recommended tour guides if in doubt. The following two recommendations cover all the main sights to be seen and explored in and around the city.

Cracow City Tours
pl. Matejki 2; tel: 12 421 1333; www.cracowcitytours.com; daily 7.30am–8.30pm; tram: 2, 4, 5, 12; map p.133 D4
One of the better and more established tour guide companies with a proper office and positive feedback about their services. They can take you on all the major tours, including Wieliczka and Auschwitz, using experts in their respective fields.

Crazy Guides
Tel: 500 09 12 00; www.crazyguides.com
A major success story in alternative guided tours with a personal touch, Crazy Guides provide a range of insightful guided tours of Nowa Huta and the steelworks in a lovingly restored Trabant 601.

Below: a river cruise on the Wisła.

Atlas

The following streetplan of Kraków makes it easy to find the attractions listed in the A–Z section. A selective index to streets and sights will help you find other locations throughout the city.

Map Legend

	Pedestrian area	✈ ✈	Airport / airfield
	Notable building	🚌	Bus station
	Park	❶	Tourist information
	Hotel	✚	Hospital
	Shopping area	🛈	Windmill
	Transport hub	⌁	Lighthouse
	Urban area	⊟	Cathedral / church
	Non urban area	✡	Synagogue
† Y	Cemetery	🎭	Theatre
═══	Railway	🯄	Statue / monument
}┈┈{	Tunnel	◔	Cave
─ ─ ─	Ferry route	✉	Post Office

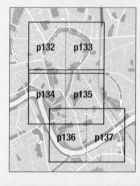

p132   p133

p134   p135

p136   p137

p132 p133
p134 p135
p136 p137

A | **B**

Kościół Zmartwychwstania Pańskiego

Sereno-Fenn'a

Basztowa

Pomnik Lilii Wenedy

Pijarska

Kościół Karmelitów 'Na Piasku' (Carmelite Church 'On the Sands')

Biblioteka Publiczna (Public Library)

Rajska

Muzeum Ubezpieczeń

Kościół św. Kazimierza (St Casimir's)

Kościół św. Marka (St Mark's)

Pomnik gen. Kutrzeby

Pomnik A. Grottgera

Pałac Sztuki (Palace of Art)

Bagatela Teatr

Muzeum S. Wyspiańskiego w domu Szołayskich (Wyspiański Museum)

Grand

Dom Józefa Mehoffera (Józef Mehoffer House)

Bunkier Sztuki (Arts Bunker)

Saski

Krupnicza

La Fontaine

Stary Teatr (Old Theatre)

Café Redolfi

Studencka

Pałac Krzysztofory (Historical Museum of Kraków at Krzysztofory Palace)

Palac Bonerowski

Kościół św. Anny (St Anna's)

Collegium Nowodworskiego (Nowodworski College)

STARE MIASTO

Rynek Główny (Main Market Square)

Dor Jasienski

Kościół Kapucynów (Capuchin)

Jagiellonian University Museum

Collegium Maius (Maius/Great College)

Pałac Pod Baranami (Palace Under the Rams)

Sukiennice (Cloth Hall)

Pomnik A. Mickiewi

Uniwersytet Jagielloński

Collegium Physicum

Eros Bendato

Pomnik Mikołaja Kopernika

Galeria Centrum

Wieża Ratuszowa (Town Hall Tower)

Gallery of 19th-Century Polish Art

Collegium Novum

Międzynarodowe Centrum Kultury

Kościół św. Wojciecha (St Adalbert's)

Kościół św. Norberta

Pałac Zbaraskich-Wodzickich

Dom Pod Obrazem (House Under the Painting)

Ho Ryne

marsz. Józefa Piłsudskiego

Teatr PWST

Rezydent

Pałac Hutten-Czapskich (Hutten-Czapskich Palace)

Pomnik Jana Pawła II

Pałac Arcybiskupi

Kościół Niepokalanego Serca Marii i klsz św Felicijanek (Church of the Sacred Heart of the Blessed Virgin Mary and St Felicity Convent)

Pomnik kard. A. Sapiehy

Plac Wszystkich Świętych

Plac Dominik

Filharmonia (Philharmonic)

Bazylika św. Franciszka z Asyżu (Basilica of St Francis of Assisi)

Urząd Miasta Krakowa

Radisson SAS

A | 134 | **B** | 134

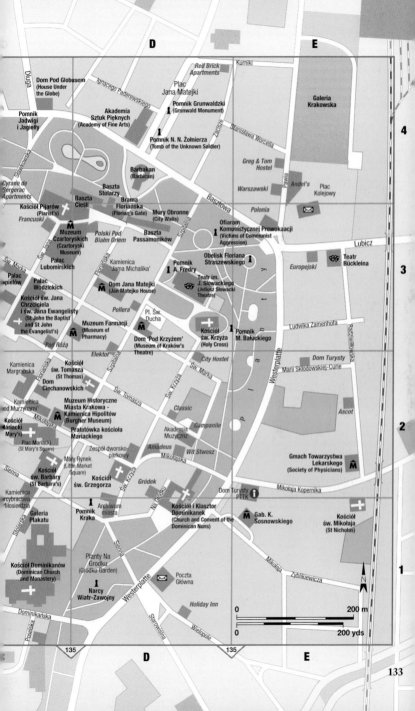

Długa

Dom Pod Globusem
(House Under
the Globe)

Ignacego Paderewskiego

Kurniki

Red Brick
Apartments

Plac
Jana Matejki

Pomnik Grunwaldzki
(Grunwald Monument)

Galeria
Krakowska

Pomnik
Jadwigi
i Jagiełły

Akademia
Sztuk Pięknych
(Academy of Fine Arts)

Stanisława Worcella

Pomnik N. N. Żołnierza
(Tomb of the Unknown Soldier)

Sławkowska

Barbakan
(Barbican)

Baszta
Stolarzy

Baszta
Cieśli

Cyrano de
Sergerac
Apartments

Brama
Floriańska
(Florian's Gate)

Basztowa

Greg & Tom
Hostel

Warszawski

Andel's

Pawia

Plac
Kolejowy

Kościół Pijarów
(Piarist's)

Francuski

Sw. Jana

Muzeum
Czartoryskich
(Czartoryski
Museum)

Polski Pod
Białm Orłem

Mury Obronne
(City Walls)

Baszta
Passamoników

Szpitalna

Ofiarom
Komunistycznej Prowokacji
(Victims of Communist
Aggression)

Polonia

Lubicz

Pałac
Lubomirskich

Sw. Marka

Pałac
Spiełów

Floriańska

Kamienica
'Jama Michalika'

Pomnik
A. Fredry

Obelisk Floriana
Straszewskiego

Europejski

Teatr
Bückleina

Pałac
Wodzickich

Dom Jana Matejki
(Jan Matejko House)

Kościół św. Jana
Chrzciciela
i św. Jana Ewangelisty
(St John the Baptist
and St John
the Evangelist's)

Pollera

Teatr im.
J. Słowackiego
(Juliusz Słowacki
Theatre)

Ludwika Zamenhofa

Radziwiłłowska

Pod Różą

Muzeum Farmacji
(Museum of
Pharmacy)

Pl. Św.
Ducha

Kościół
św. Krzyża
(Holy Cross)

Pomnik
M. Bałuckiego

Dom Turysty

Elektor

Szpitalna

Dom 'Pod Krzyżem'
(Museum of Kraków's
Theatre)

City Hostel

Sw. Marka

Marii Skłodowskiej-Curie

Kamienica
Margrabska

Floriańska

Kościół
św. Tomasza
(St Thomas)

Sw. Krzyża

Sw. Tomasza

Classic

Westerplatte

Ascot

Dom
Ciechanowskich

Kamienica
'pod Murzynami'

Muzeum Historyczne
Miasta Krakowa -
Kamienica Hipolitów
(Burgher Museum)

Campanile

Akademia
Muzyczna

Gmach Towarzystwa
Lekarskiego
(Society of Physicians)

Mikołajska

Kościół
Mariacki
Mary's)

Plac Mariacki
(St Mary's Square)

Prałatówka kościoła
Mariackiego

Zespół dworsko-
parkowy

Amadeus

Wit Stwosz

Mikołajska

Sienna

Mały Rynek
(Little Market
Square)

Sw. Krzyża

Mikołaja Kopernika

Kościół
św. Barbary
(St Barbary's)

Kościół
św. Grzegorza

Gródek

Na Gródku

Dom Turysty
PTTK

Gab. K.
Sosnowskiego

Kościół
św. Mikołaja
(St Nicholas)

Kamienica
rcybractwa
iłosierdzia

Galeria
Plakatu

Pomnik
Kraka

Archiwum
miasta

Kościół i Klasztor
Dominikanek
(Church and Convent of the
Dominican Nuns)

Mikołaja

Zyblikiewicza

Stolarska

Sienna

Planty Na
Grodku
(Gródku Garden)

Westerplatte

Poczta
Główna

Kościół Dominikanów
(Dominican Church
and Monastery)

Narcy
Wiatr-Zawojny

Holiday Inn

0   200 m

0   200 yds

Pasiaska

Dominikańska

Starowiślna

Wielopole

N

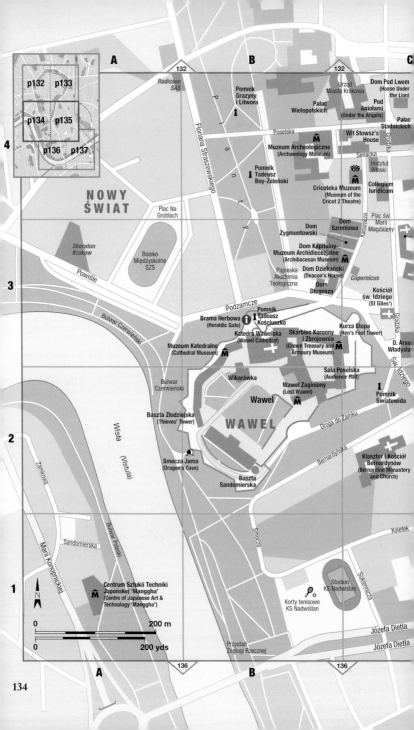

Radisson SAS

Pomnik Grazyny i Litwora

Urząd Miasta Krakowa

Dom Pod Lwem (House Under the Lion)

Pałac Wielopolskich

Pod Aniołami (Under the Angels)

Pałac Stadnickich

Poselska

Wit Stowsz's House

Muzeum Archeologiczne (Archaeology Museum)

Senacka

Instytut Włoski

Pomnik Tadeusz Boy-Żeleński

Cricoteka Muzeum (Museum of the Cricot 2 Theatre)

Collegium Iuridicum

NOWY ŚWIAT

Plac Na Groblach

Dom Zygmuntowski

Dom Szreniawa

Plac św. Marii Magdaleny

Sheraton Kraków

Boisko Międzyskolne SZS

Dom Kapitulny – Muzeum Archidiecezjalne (Archdiocesan Museum)

Powiśle

Papieska Akademia Teologiczna

Dom Dziekański (Deacon's House)

Copernicus

Dom Długosza

Kościół św. Idziego (St Giles')

Podzamcze

Bulwar Czerwieński

Pomnik Tadeusz Kościuszko

Brama Herbowa (Heraldic Gate)

Kurza Stopa (Hen's Foot Tower)

Katedra Wawelska (Wawel Cathedral)

Skarbiec Koronny i Zbrojownia (Crown Treasury and Armoury Museum)

D. Arsen Władysła

Muzeum Katedralne (Cathedral Museum)

Wikarówka

Sala Poselska (Audience Hall)

Bulwar Czerwieński

Wawel Zaginiony (Lost Wawel)

Pomnik Światowida

Baszta Złodziejska (Thieves' Tower)

Wawel

WAWEL

Wisła (Mistula)

Droga do Zamku

Bernardyńska

Smocza Jama (Dragon's Cave)

Baszta Sandomierska

Klasztor i Kościół Bernardynów (Bernardine Monastery and Church)

Zamkowa

Smocza

Koletek

Sandomierska

Bulwar Podłeki

Centrum Sztukii Techniki Japońskiej 'Mangha' (Centre of Japanese Art & Technology 'Mangha')

Stadion KS Nadwiślan

Szklennicza

Marii Konopnickiej

Korty tenisowe KS Nadwiślan

Józefa Dietla

N

0   200 m

0   200 yds

Przystań Żeglugi Rzecznej

Józefa Dietla

Floriana Straszewskiego

133

Bonerowska

Wielkopole

Pożegka

Wawel-
Tourist

Kościół
sw. Józefa
(St Joseph's)

Sw. Gertrudy

Liborowszczyzna

Pałac
Pugetów

Starowiślna

Józefa Dietla

Józefa Dietla

D. Klasztor
Jezuitów

Scena
Kameralna

Kościół św. Piotra
i Pawła
(St Peter and St Paul's)

Kameralny

Józefa Sarego

Wrześińska

Kościół św.
Andrzeja Apostoła
(St Andrew the Apostle's)

Wojciecha Bogusławskiego

Kościół św. Marcina
(St Martin's)

Sw. Sebastiana

Garnizonowy

Sw. Gertrudy

Muzeum Przyrodnicze
(Natural History Museum and Aquarium)

Sw. Sebastiana

Royal

Starowiślna

Berka Joselewicza

STRADOM

Berka Joselewicza

Plac
ernardyński

Brzozowa

Kościół Księży Misjonarzy
(Church of the
Missionary Priests)

Podbrzezie

Landau's
House

Józefa Dietla

Józefa Dietla

Klezmer
Hois

Stradomska

Synagoga Tempel
(Tempel Synagogue)

Miodowa

CMENTARZ

Steroka

Pomnik Ofiar
Holocaustu

Sw. Agnieszki

Bożnica Kupa
(Kupa Synagogue)

Synagoga Remuh
(Remuh Synagogue)

Aparthotel
Spatz

Jonatana Warszauera

REMUH

former Popper
Synagogue

Nathan's
Villa Hostel

Franciszek

Estery

Kolory
B & B

Jakuba

Steroka

Dawna rytualna
rzeźnia żydowska
(former Jewish ritual
slaughterhouse)

Plac Nowy

Kupa

Eden

Rubinstein

Kościół
św. Agnieszki

Miodowa

Synagoga Izaaka
(Isaac Synagogue)

Na Górce Synagogue

Kazimierz's
Secret

Kazimierz Market

Izaaka

Stara Synagoga
(Old Synagogue)

Bożego Ciała

Tournet

Centrum Kultury
Żydowskiej
(Jewish Cultural Centre)

Plac Nowy

Estery

Nowa

Astoria

Karmel

Plac Bawół

Krakowska

Former Wysoka
Bożnica
(High Synagogue)

Museum of Jewish
History
and Culture

Augustiańska

Meiselsa

Regent

Józefa

Wąska

KAZIMIERZ

137

137

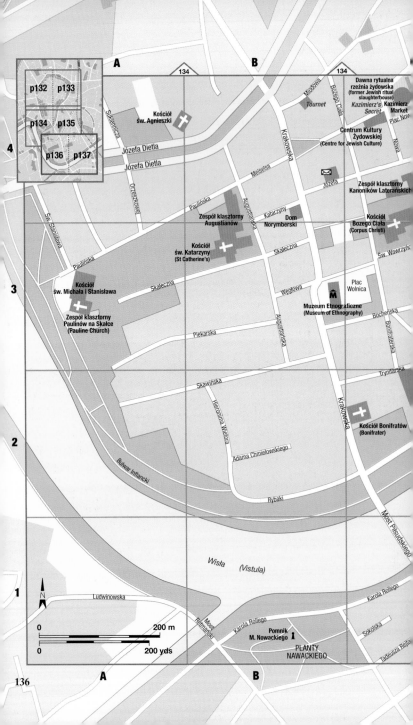

Dawna rytualna
rzeźnia żydowska
(former Jewish ritual
slaughterhouse)
Kazimierz's Kazimierz
Secret Market
Plac Nov

Tournet

Miłowa

Bożego Ciała

Krakowska

Plac Now

Centrum Kultury
Żydowskiej
(Centre for Jewish Culture)

Nowa

Kościół
św. Agnieszki

Sukiennica

Józefa Dietla

Józefa Dietla

Meiselsa

Józefa

Zespół klasztorny
Kanoników Laterańskich

Orzeszkowej

Paulińska

Augustiańska

Katarzyny

Dom
Norymberski

Kościół
Bożego Ciała
(Corpus Christi)

św. Stanisława

Zespół klasztorny
Augustianów

Kościół
św. Katarzyny
(St Catherine's)

Skałeczna

Św. Wawrzyńc

Paulińska

Kościół
św. Michała i Stanisława

Skałeczna

Węglowa

Plac
Wolnica

Bocheńska

Zespół klasztorny
Paulinów na Skałce
(Pauline Church)

Muzeum Etnograficzne
(Museum of Ethnography)

Piekarska

Augustiańska

Bonifraterska

Trynitarska

Skawińska

Hieronima Wielra

Krakowska

Kościół Bonifratów
(Bonifrater)

Bulwar Inflancki

Adama Chmielowskiego

Rybaki

Most Piłsudskiego

Wisła   (Vistula)

Karola Rollego

N

Ludwinowska

Most Retmański

Karola Rollego

Pomnik
M. Nowackiego

PLANTY
NAWACKIEGO

Sokolska

Tadeusza Rejta

0   200 m

0   200 yds

p132	p133
p134	p135
p136	p137

4

3

2

1

D
E

4

lory
& B
Synagoga Izaaka
(Isaac Synagogue)

Eden

Szeroka

Rubinstein

Na Górce Synagogue

Kupa

Jakuba

Stara Synagoga
(Old Synagogue)

zaaka

Karmel

Józefa

Former Wysoka
Bóżnica
(High Synagogue)

Plac
Bawół

Museum of Jewish
History and Culture

storia

KAZIMIERZ

Wąska

Bartosza

Dajwór

Galicia
Jewish Museum

Przemyska

Halicka

Św. Wawrzyńca

Starowiślna

Św. Wawrzyńca

Gazowa

Muzeum Inżynierii
Miejskiej
(City Engineering
Museum)

Podgórska

3

Mostowa

Bulwar Kurlandzki

Podgórska

Most Powstańców Śląskich

Miesiowa

Szpital Zakonu
Bonifratrów

Podgórska

Port Solny

Nadwiślańska

Solna

Plac
Bohaterów
Getta

Na Zjeździe

Qubus

Solna

Piwna

2

Nadwiślańska

Piwna

Targowa

Plac
Bohaterów Getta
(Ghetto Heroes' Square,
former Plac Zgody)

Muzeum Pamięci
Narodowej
(Museum of National
Remembrance)

Krakusa

Józefińska

Józefińska

Kazimierza Brodzińskiego

PODGÓRZE

czy Moście

Staromostowa

Węgierska

Al. Bolesława Limanowskiego

1

Celna

Al. Bolesława Limanowskiego

Tynek Podgórski

Rynek Podgórski

Town
Hall

Węgierska

Galeria
Rękawka
& Podgórze
Museum

Krakusa

Św. Benedykta

Czarnieckiego

egionów

Legionów

Starmach Gallery
(former Zucher's
Synagogue)

D
E

Street Atlas Index

Index

Bars and Cafés

Hotels

Restaurants

Insight Smart Guide: Kraków

Compiled by: **Richard Schofield**

Edited by: **Sarah Sweeney**
Proofread and indexed by: **Neil Titman**

Photography by: **Alamy** 85, 96, 97, 98, 101, 113, 128; **Andel's** 71; **Baccarat** 95; **Christophe Boisvieux/Corbis** 128; **Boom Bar Rush** 94/95; **Verity Borthwick** 36/37; **Tim Brakemeier/epa/Corbis** 59; **Peter Clark/fotoLibra** 45, 53; **Copernicus** 67, 110; **Drukarnia** 37; **Forum/Reuters/Corbis** 76; **Fotolia** 11T&B; **Kevin Foy/Rex Features** 121; **Groteska Theatre, Great Dragons' Parade** 56/57, 120; **David Harding/fotoLibra** 20; **Hemis/Axiom** 92/93; **Guillaume Horcajuelo/epa/Corbis** 58; **Hotel Amadeus** 66; **iStockphoto.com** 3B, 21B, 51B, 57; **Karmel** 69L; **Jama Michalika** 33; **Henryk T. Kaiser/Rex Features** 17B, 118/119; **Raphaël Labbé** 76/77; **Manggha Museum** 14; **Jan Mehlich** 21T; **Miejsce** 3CRB, 35; **Miod i Wino** 105B; **Monopol** 73; **Ogniem i Meczziem** 109T; **Pod Baranem** 109B; **Pod Krzyzkiem** 102; **Qubus Hotel** 66/67; **Radisson SAS** 72; **robche02** 99; **Rubinstein** 69R; **Krzysztof Rymarczyk/Krakow Academy of Music** 92; **Superstock** 10, 46; **Tips Images** 2B, 83, 87T;

TopFoto 58/59, 65R; **Tournet** 70; **Corrie Wingate/APA** 2T, 3CL, C&CRT, 4B, 5, 6, 7T&B, 8, 9T&B, 13T&B, 15T&B, 16, 17T, 19T&B, 22, 23T&B, 24/25, 26/27(all), 28/29(all), 31T&B, 32, 34T, 38, 39, 40, 42, 43, 48, 49, 50T, 51, 52/53, 54/55, 60, 62B, 68, 74/75(all), 78, 79, 80/81(all), 82, 82/83, 84T&B, 86, 87B, 88, 89, 90, 91, 100, 100/101, 104, 107, 108, 112, 112/113, 114/115(all), 116, 117L&R, 119, 120/121, 122, 122/123, 124, 125B, 126/127(all); **Gregory Wrona/APA** 3T, 4T, 12, ‟ 32/33, 34B, 36, 38/39, 40/41, 42/43, 44, 47, 52, 55, 60/61, 61, 62T, 63, 78/79, 94, 102/103, 103, 105T, 106, 111, 118, 123, 125T, 129T, 130/131; **Craig Wyzik** 41

Picture Manager: **Steven Lawrence**
Maps: **James Macdonald**
Series Editor: **Jason Mitchell**

First Edition 2010

© 2010 Apa Publications GmbH & Co. Verlag KG Singapore Branch, Singapore.

Worldwide distribution enquiries:
Apa Publications GmbH & Co. Verlag KG (Singapore Branch) 38 Joo Koon Road, Singapore 628990; tel: (65) 6865 1600; e-mail: apasin@singnet.com.sg

Distributed in the UK and Ireland by:
GeoCenter International Ltd
Meridian House, Churchill Way West, Basingstoke, Hampshire RG21 6YR; tel: (44 1256) 817 987; e-mail: sales@geocenter.co.uk

Distributed in the United States by:
Langenscheidt Publishers, Inc.
36–36 33rd Street 4th Floor, Long Island City, New York 11106; tel: (1 718) 784 0055; e-mail: orders@langenscheidt.com

Contacting the Editors
We would appreciate it if readers would alert us to outdated information by writing to:
Apa Publications, PO Box 7910, London SE1 1WE, UK; fax: (44 20) 7403 0290; e-mail: insight@apaguide.co.uk

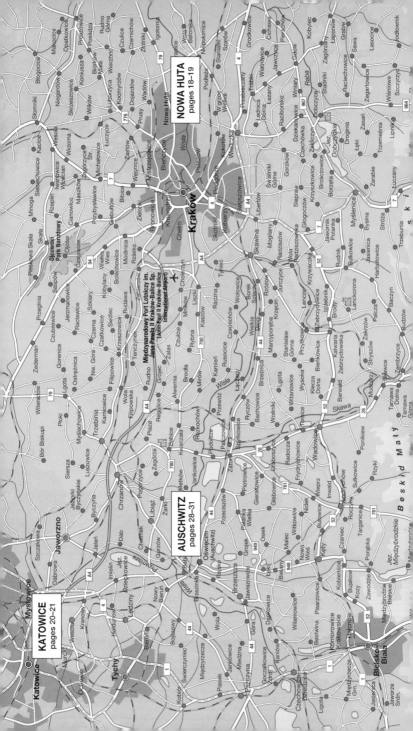